Acknowledgments

The Age of Selfishness by Martin Jacques © Martin Jacques and *Up Front this Much I Know* by Simon Garfield © Simon Garfield, by permission of Guardian Newspaper Limited. *The Confessions of St Augustine* trans & intro by E M Blaiklock, by permission of Hodder and Stoughton Limited. *The Dignity of Difference* by Jonathan Sacks, by permission of Continuum International Publishing Limited. *Intimacy and the Hungers* of the Heart by Pat Collins and *Passion for the Possible* by Daniel J O'Leary, by permission of Columba Press. *New Seeds of Contemplation* by Thomas Merton © 1961, The Abbey of Gethsemani Inc. *The Asian Journals of Thomas Merton* by Thomas Merton © Thomas Merton 1975 by The Thomas Merton Legacy Trust, by permission of New Directions Publishing Corporation. *Wellsprings* by Anthony De Mello, by permission of Random House Inc. *The Strength of the Weak* by Dorothee Soelle, by permission of SPCK/WJK Press. *Spirituality and Theology* by Philip Sheldrake ©1998 and *Clashing Symbols*, by Michael Paul Gallagher ©1997 and *Jerusalem Bible* ©1985 by permission of Darton Longman & Todd. *Vita Consecrata,* from Vatican Document ©Libreria Editrice Vaticana with their permission. *The Changing Face of Priesthood* by Frank Cozzens, by permission of The Liturgical Press. Teihard de Chardin quote "There is no 'Within' without a 'Without' there is no 'Without' without a 'Within'" quoted in Donald Georgen's article published in Dominican Ashram June 2001, by permission of Dominican Publications India Private Limited. *Prayer and the Quest for Healing* and *Wrestling With God* by Barbara Fiand and *Simplicity* by Richard Rohr, by permission of The Crossroad Publishing Company. *Releasement* by Barbara Fiand, by kind permission of the Author. Femininity *Lost And Regained* by Robert A Johnson, Harper Perrennial. *The Fisher King and the Handless Maiden* by Robert A Johnson, Harper San Francisco. *Owning your own Shadow* by Robert A Johnson, Harper San Francisco, by permission of Harper Collins New York. *Touching the Face of God* by Donna Tiernan Mahoney, by permission of Mercier Press.

We have made every effort to contact copyright holders and seek their permission to use their material. If any involuntary infringement of copyright has occurred, we offer our apologies and will correct any error in future editions. The *Heroine's Journey* by Maureen Murdoch ©1990 reprinted by arrangement with Shambhala Publications Inc Boston, www.shambhala.com

ISBN 0-9544539-0-5

© Don Bosco Publications

Don Bosco Publications
Thornleigh House
Bolton BL1 6PQ
Tel 01204 308811

© 2003 Michael J Cunningham

Dedicated to the memory of my parents

Contents

Introduction

There is no 'within' without a 'without'
and no 'without' without a 'within' [1]

For the last three summers I have been involved in retreats across the USA with my Salesian brothers and sisters. I thank them warmly for their encouragement and advice. Many of the ideas in this book began as retreat talks and have been refined and re-written for this publication. Much of the specifically Salesian material has been omitted, to address the wider questions which face apostolic religious life in the newly emerging post-modern environment.

Judged by external criteria, religious life in the western world appears to be in decline. Numbers are down, the age profile is increasingly high, and works are being closed or passed on to lay leadership. Rather than bemoan these changes I think they are in fact part of God's purpose in asking us to re-think and re-imagine religious life in a more radical way. It is our invitation to live the Paschal Mystery, which is the pattern for all Christian spirituality. Too many of us, in the Catholic Church, prefer the private journey.

Throughout history, and in many cultures, there have been men and women called to live the deepest values of the culture. Religious life belongs to this liminal tradition and its purpose is to remind all of us that our essential humanity can be discovered only in the quest for God, which is in fact God's quest and love for us. Thus the individual journey of the religious only makes sense as a communal quest.

It is the argument of this book that we are all suffering from a serious imbalance between the inner, more reflective aspects of our humanity, and our outer and more active lives. This is true of the culture as it is of religious life and is damaging to the health and vitality of both. Our postmodern world has rejected the myths of modernity. We cannot continue to read reality through the narrow lens of science and technology. The dazzling successes of technology have come at a high price for our humanity. This price is being paid in our souls, in our inner lives. We lack meaning and a common vision; we are left with the loneliness of a rather rugged individualism, which has become the great myth of the West. Not surprisingly it is being rejected in the poorer parts of our world.

---

[1] Teilhard de Chardin quoted in article by Donald Georgen
(published in Dominican Ashram June 2001)

In chapter one I try to situate the current crisis in religious life within the wider crisis of our postmodern world, which appears indifferent to God yet at the same time in search of deeper meaning. Rather than see woundedness and brokeness as failure we are being challenged to new and more radical growth. Chapter two examines how part of the crisis we face is due to a lack of harmony between the outer masculine journey and the inner feminine journey. A healthy spirituality has to be androgynous, incorporating both masculine and feminine dimensions of our humanity. The third chapter looks at how our culture, religious and secular, is slowly being drawn to a more relational model as we seek a healthier balance.

This shift from the rational left-brain thinking to a more holistic right-brain understanding is explored in myths and stories in chapter four, in the search for a more symbolic and unified perspective. Myths are crucial in that they summon the hero/heroine figure in us all and they move our lives beyond the individualism of the West into a deeper and more embracing communal story. Their use of *both/and* rather than *either/or* thinking leads to an inclusive rather than merely competitive vision. This shift requires a much better integration of the feminine with the overtly masculine world in which we all currently live.

Chapter five argues that this wisdom cannot be found in a kind of angelic spirituality of perfection but is discovered only in the radical journey within and the radical journey without, one that accepts and gets close to human poverty, brokeness and woundedness. Nor can it be found in the postmodern cult of celebrity. The fascination projected onto public celebrity figures suppresses the hero/heroine within us all. In the Church and in religious life this kind of projection has often led to an unreal spirituality of perfection, even a distorted view of sanctity.

The essential limitations of our human condition have to be included not excluded from this journey as the hero and the heroine return to share the wisdom of their wounds with the community. Chapter six, therefore, considers community not so much in ideal but in real terms as a place for owning the darker aspects of our shadow life. Community then becomes a school where our human joys and sorrows invite us to live a spirituality of compassion and forgiveness.

The final three chapters look at the vows as essential resources in creating a better balance between the within and the without. The key insight is that religious life needs to address the radical need for intimacy, as modelled for us by Jesus in the Gospels. This intimacy has to own all aspects of the self, good and bad, light and dark. In chapter seven I try to present a more positive, relational view of consecrated celibacy as a way to intimacy with others rather than avoidance. Chapter eight extends this intimacy to our inner selves, uncovering a poverty in spirit which opens us to a deep need for prayer and an intimacy with God which is foundational for a spirituality of the heart.

The inner journey is not meant to take us away from the essential aspect of mission in apostolic religious life. On the contrary it provides a new stimulus to live our vow of obedience in a way which challenges us to plan and work together in a renewed intimacy with our postmodern world. In this way we are led to share the joys and sorrows of others by dedicated service.

The vow of obedience takes us back into the outer world of mission not as independent individuals, but in a humbler more collaborative style, one that seeks to meet the hungers of our age. As religious, we challenge our postmodern world and ourselves to a wider reading of the signs of the times, one that embraces the radical relatedness of all human beings, especially the stranger. We humbly share the wisdom of our wounds as our lives move between the radical journey within and the radical journey without and discover that the two journeys become one.

Finally I wish to thank my Salesian brothers who have inspired me in my years of religious life. I have suffered with them and laughed with them. I am very conscious that everything I write stems from a masculine and limited point of view. So I also wish to thank and acknowledge my women friends, many of them in religious life, who have taught me real courage and a sense of delight in the enchanted yet flawed world in which we live. Their faces are hidden in the text of my story.

Michael Cunningham
Feast of the Epiphany 2003

CHAPTER ONE

Religious Life at Ground Zero

As on the day of the assassination of President Kennedy, most of us remember what we were doing on September 11th 2001 when the terrorist attack destroyed the Twin Towers in New York City. First impressions that this might be an accident soon turned to shock and incomprehension as the full horror and scale of the tragedy sank in. In the ensuing days people compared the dramatic television footage to Hollywood disaster films. This was no fantasy; it was real and the raw emotions of the families of victims mingled on our television screens with the inspiring courage of the rescue workers.

Six months after the tragedy I found myself taking a short journey from our Salesian parish in East 12th Street New York City down to the area which had become known to the world as Ground Zero. It was Holy Saturday. The cold of early spring was turning into a warm Easter weekend. I travelled with very mixed emotions. New York has always been an attractive city for tourists. The danger now is that Ground Zero becomes yet another site to tick off in the list of places to see: Statue of Liberty, Central Park, and now Ground Zero. To control the number of visitors the city authorities had set up a system of tickets to get access to the viewing area. I declined this option and simply took a bus down Broadway and then walked to the edge of the site where St Paul's Church stands. The empty space where the majestic towers had once stood was eloquent testimony to what had happened.

At the time of the disaster St Paul's Church had opened its doors to the many rescue workers. These men and women laboured far beyond the call of duty to recover the remains of fallen comrades and office workers. On this warm Holy Saturday afternoon the streets were filled with onlookers gazing at the many pictures of the dead, solidarity slogans, and American flags which were still attached to the railings along the sidewalk. Outside the church people were praying and singing hymns. The atmosphere seemed very conducive to the strange mixture of emotions that Holy Saturday brings: sadness at the death of Christ gradually giving way to the hope and joy of the Resurrection.

During the next couple of months, while giving a series of retreats to the Salesian Sisters, I made a number of visits to New York City. Over many years I have come to love the city, I even count myself a supporter of the New York Yankees baseball team. But the city has always had a reputation for brashness and arrogance. It is a city with a hard edge that has promoted celebrity and success. Every Yankees ball game ends with the voice of Frank Sinatra booming out 'New York, New York.....if I can make it there I'll make it anywhere.'

It is not a city easily associated with humility, with vulnerability, with brokeness. Yet since the dramatic events of 9/11 the place has undoubtedly changed. The tragedy brought about a new spirit of solidarity and compassion. The city rediscovered itself. Where celebrity and success had been worshipped, people began to appreciate the heroism of its ordinary unsung workers: its fire-fighters and police, and its chaplains. Where the individualism of the yuppie culture had once reigned supreme there was a new appreciation of the values of shared togetherness and community.

Waiting at Newark airport as I left New York to fly back to England I glanced again at the new skyline of the city. Still awe-inspiring in its majesty yet with a new vulnerability. Its very woundedness seemed to be giving it a new identity. My thoughts turned to the more familiar landscape of my own life: the life of a male religious priest at the threshold of a new millennium. As the lights of Manhattan disappeared into the night sky, and we headed across the Atlantic, I reflected on the changes that had occurred, and were still unfolding in the religious life I had embraced so enthusiastically, and perhaps naively, some 38 years previously. The day after I was clothed in the cassock, as a Salesian novice, President Kennedy was shot. In 1964 I was one of a group of 24 novices. Now, not only does my province have no novices, like so many others, we have no one in the whole period of initial formation. As I headed home on that long transatlantic flight, I found myself ruminating on what the future might bring.

Apparent Decline

Anyone surveying religious life in the western world at a superficial level, would find it difficult to see signs of encouragement. Religious life appears to be wounded and in decline. In recent years many orders and congregations involved in traditional ministries, such as teaching and nursing, have found themselves reduced in numbers and increasingly handing over to lay leadership, or closing down. Large houses are giving way to smaller ones. One of the few growth areas seems to be finding ways of caring for elderly religious who are no longer directly involved in ministry.

In our very pragmatic world everything is subject to testing and analysis. We value what can be measured. We place so much importance on quantity. Politicians throw numbers around like confetti in terms of more money, more teachers, more doctors and nurses, more policemen on the beat. Despite this there is often an unease felt by the general public who sense that somehow *more* doesn't always mean *better*.

All too easily the Church can also get drawn into the numbers game. When you meet religious superiors today, understandably you will hear them speak of the need for more vocations. At some time in the future, and by God's grace and our renewed lives, that new influx may well happen. However I suspect that this *solution* may well mask a deeper problem. The more I reflect on what is happening to our western religious life, the more I am convinced that we may well have to learn to go deeper into our contemporary experience, and learn to live with its darkness and with its woundedness. As the citizens of New York stared into the abyss of Ground Zero it offered them an opportunity to reflect on a whole way of life that was being massively rejected by a different culture. An opportunity which not everyone wanted to take.

Asking questions, seeking understanding, is a long and difficult process and in a culture that demands instant solutions we can become trapped into repeating the patterns of the past. This inability to think outside the box, to use our imaginations, to grapple with difficult problems, and the lack of a compelling vision that can see beyond the immediate needs is a symptom of a crisis that faces our civilisation.

A Shared Crisis

I am becoming convinced that the very woundedness and weakness that we encounter, our inability to *fix* the world cannot be ignored. Maybe it can provide some new growth that will lead to a deeper and more holistic response. The bible reminds us that the rejected stone becomes the cornerstone of the new building. The whole mystery of the Cross and Resurrection, the Paschal Mystery, sums up the spiritual life and yet we seem to look for success in terms of numbers and growth. Sandra Schneiders has suggested that religious life is corporately going through what John of the Cross identified in the individual spiritual journey as the dark night of the soul:

> **The cultural cataclysm that many analysts are beginning to call the transition from modernity to postmodernity is functioning in the lives of many religious in a way analogous to the purifying trials of the interior life that John describes apropos of the enclosed contemplative.[2]**

Rather than be depressed by this I think it can lead to a new kind of dialogue with secular society undergoing its own crisis of meaning. Under the brash confidence of consumer capitalism lies a real unease and restlessness. A strategic marketing consultant offers this revealing comment:

> **If you want to invest in anything invest in religion. I don't know how you do that, unfortunately. But people do have a sense there's something missing in their lives.[3]**

The problem is that late modernity has left us with the apparent triumph of technical reason which tries to reduce every problem to a manageable solution while leaving the underlying crisis untouched. Every problem can be solved by yet another action plan! While the action plans unfold, society seems to be fragmenting. We need more than a quick fix.

The Postmodern Challenge

The crisis of western civilisation has been well documented in recent years. In our postmodern world all institutions that carried and conveyed meaning to the next generation are now regarded with increasing scepticism, especially by the younger generation. In the UK, the monarchy, parliament, politicians, clergy, journalists and teachers consistently score low marks in polls that record public attitudes. The fact that these groups are communicators of cultural values reveals the depth of the problem. Their places in the old intelligentsia seem to have been usurped by celebrities, television and film stars, pop stars and entertainers.

---

[2] Sandra Schneiders *Contemporary Religious life: Death or Transformation?* in *Religious Life: the Challenge for Tomorrow* edited by Cassian J Yuhaus (N Y Mahwah Paulist Press 1994) p18

[3] Martin Hayward *This Much I Know* (Observer Magazine London Dec 29th 2002) p 6

On a positive note there appear to be signs of convergence as commentators seek to uncover what can only be described as the religious and spiritual roots at the heart of the cultural crisis. The arguments about how to live, in the world of modernity, centred on the kind of society we create. This question quickly got reduced to competing theories about economics. On the one hand we had the monolithic blocks of communist states; on the other the more open societies created by western capitalism. With the collapse of Communism, the West seems to have won the argument decisively and some even put forward the case for the end of history. Global capitalism now has the chance to penetrate all the markets of the world. Ideology is now of little concern; the only political question is how to manage the system. All political parties have embraced managerialism; political vision is out.

The triumph of global capitalism has not brought about unbridled happiness. The dominance of managerial and technical values has received criticism from those who look for a more compelling vision. Internationally global capitalism seems unable to address the crisis of world poverty. At national level the triumph of market forces seems to create societies with a high crime rate and a weakening of community bonds and values, and a loss of meaning. While a wide variety of sexual lifestyles is tolerated, and morality reduced to a question of personal opinion, the undermining of the family as the basic building block of society seems to gather pace.

Vatican II asked all of us to read and discern the signs of the times. Increasingly commentators are underlining the weakening of social and community ties. In a perceptive article on the state of contemporary Britain, Martin Jacques, former editor of Marxism Today, describes the lack of balance that exists in our lives. We work far longer hours than any European country and therefore have less time for family, for friends, in other words for relationships. All the emphasis seems to be placed on personal freedom at the expense of family and community responsibilities. Jacques underlines some of the consequences of this lack of harmony:

All have suffered grievous harm in the face of the advancing army of personal freedom. We may live in the age of freedom, but it should more properly be described as an age of

selfishness. The result is the myriad ties that hold society together have been seriously weakened.[4]

The Cultural Crisis is a Spiritual Crisis

In a preface to the revised edition of an earlier book Joe Holland claims:

Our whole Western civilisation has entered into a profound and irreversible crisis.[5]

He suggests that the word *civilisation* is a more helpful word than *society*. That is because it includes and adds the word culture to the rather narrow flat reduction of society to economic and market forces. Holland suggests, in a revealing insight, that it is:

This question of culture, and within it *religion* (my italics), **which reveals, I believe, the most radical dimension of our social crisis.**[6]

He links the creative and critical energy that drives culture to its participation in divine creativity. At the heart of a culture's civilisation is the Holy Spirit, the divine wind that swept over the waters of creation. This insight has been built on by a much richer theological understanding of creation theology that sees God's creative energy and love at the heart of our world.

Commentators on the social and political scene, on what might be called our outer life, are looking for a more holistic paradigm to understand what is happening to us. The twentieth century also witnessed a rapid growth and interest in our inner lives. Carl Jung concluded that the roots of every problem with which he was confronted in his clients in the second half of life were religious and spiritual. It seems that in whatever direction our future lies it needs to include a better balance between the outer and the inner life, between the *within* and the *without*. This is the main theme that I want to address in this book.

The Response of Religious

The Second Vatican Council made a strong link between Gospel and culture, uniting in a single vision its theological understanding of Church in Lumen Gentium with its cultural understanding of the contemporary world

---

[4] Martin Jacques *The Age of Selfishness* (The Guardian October 5th 2002)
[5] Joe Holland *Social Analysis* (N Y Maryknoll Orbis Books 1990 Preface) p xii
[6] *Social Analysis* p xii

in Gaudium et Spes. But Vatican II was a child of its time and the 1960s was undoubtedly a period of human optimism. I can still recall the excitement and promise of those days of the Council and its aftermath when I was a young religious. The work of renewal in liturgy, in ecclesiology, and in religious life seemed to offer such promise. No group entered into the renewal project with more energy than religious. Since then we have had re-written constitutions, endless chapters and planning processes. As the documentation has mounted, the world's trees have barely survived the demand for paper.

It is easy to be cynical about all this. That is not what I am saying. We have all participated in many of these processes, and much good has been done. Looking back, however, I think we would have to admit that we are still struggling with what Vatican II identified as the most serious issue of our times: the division between faith and life. Unfortunately, just as the Church was learning to turn towards the world with optimism and a sense of dialogue, the whole project of *modernity* was on the edge of collapse. As the Church was moving from its pre-Vatican II defensiveness to a more open dialogue, the world was no longer interested; it had apparently moved on to other concerns.

When I began teaching Religious Education in Liverpool in the 1970s I could still engage in challenging discussions with some pupils. Now, as we move further into the 21st century, I meet far more indifference than opposition. For too long we have been providing answers to questions that no one is asking anymore. We have arrived for the voyage to find that the boat has already left the shore. I can recall arriving at a church one Sunday morning in Bootle, Merseyside. I wasn't too sure of my directions. Some boys playing football in the street recognised me as their RE teacher. They walked me to the church in a very friendly fashion as we discussed the fortunes of Liverpool and Everton football clubs. As I reached the door to go in to celebrate the Eucharist, they all bolted in the opposite direction!

That small event was quite a significant moment for me, as a religious, who had joined the Salesians of Don Bosco in the confident days of Vatican II. In the heady days of the 60s and 70s I was happy to embrace the changes introduced by the Council. Religious life was opening up to a bright and prosperous future. The various changes couldn't come quickly enough, as far as I was concerned. We were at the beginning of a new springtime. The Catholic Church, my Church, was embracing the modern world. Progressive theology seemed to be winning the arguments, and a more liberal future offered all kinds of possibilities.

Looking back at religious life from that vantage point, most of my generation were happy to leave behind the conservative values, that had kept an unbreakable grip on religious life and ecclesial life for so long. The liturgy was now in English and the celebrant faced the people; in religious life superiors consulted their members, who were even being asked to contribute their views on all kinds of things. There was more freedom and the opportunity to engage in discussion about the future.

However, the disquieting signs were already present. As religious life moved from a predominantly conservative to a more liberal model, a number of our companions began to leave. It is impossible to generalise as to the range of motives for this haemorrhaging, but I think it was the first wounding experience for me in religious life. The people who left were often those I admired, saw as friends, and in some cases even heroes. At the same time, as we were reaching the end of the twentieth century, the numbers leaving were not being replaced by new blood. Religious life throughout the western world seemed to be in a spiral of decline.

During this period of numerical decline, religious leaders have continued to urge their members to strive to do all they can to increase the number of vocations. One former provincial remarked that there is hardly an initiative that can be thought of that hasn't been tried by sincere and hard-working religious during these years of decline. We have tried prayer, vigils, novenas, study days, vocation camps, vocation exhibitions; we have invited prospective candidates to share our community life, we have offered invitations to all and sundry, but all to little effect. There is a weariness at times among good priests and religious at the latest call for more initiatives:

They point to the paucity of serious theological reflection among church leaders on the dearth of vocations to the priesthood and religious life. Instead strategies for more effective recruitment

by vocation directors and parish priests are discussed while Catholics are urged to pray for vocations. As important as these initiatives are they distract from the hard creative and analytical thinking demanded by the present situation.[7]

Clearly these initiatives need to be tried, but I do think that we have to start asking some deeper and more serious questions about why it is, that as we have opened our renewal process to the liberal agenda, dynamic young people with idealism and energy are not inclined to join what we are modelling. At the same time we need to ask more seriously how we can model a more lay and less clerical church.

The Problem of Efficiency

In the run up to the 1995 synod on religious life, the results of an extensive survey of around 10,000 religious were published.[8] One of its conclusions found that most religious were unaware of how deeply they were affected by the culture in which they lived. This has profound significance for religious life in the western world, because we live in a capitalist culture. It is a culture that places exaggerated stress upon work. Our lives are dominated by doing things, by ceaseless activity. Whatever we achieve, it is never quite good enough. More must be done. When asked by a journalist to identify the greatest spiritual disease of our time, Thomas Merton answered with one word: *efficiency*. An extraverted culture usually leads to an extraverted spirituality. His point was that keeping the system running efficiently drained so much energy and time. It is not that people are bad; they are just exhausted!

There is a price to be paid for this excessive and restless activity. This price is being paid in our inner lives. A healthy spirituality needs a sense of balance. We have to find ways of marrying the active and necessary part of our lives with our inner world, the world of rest, of reflection, of prayer and of contemplation. I think that religious life has an important contribution to make here.

---

[7] Donald B Cozzens *The Changing Face Of The Priesthood*
(The Liturgical Press Collegeville Minnesota 2000) p19

[8] David J Nygren & Miriam D Ukeritis *Transforming Tradition: Shaping the Mission and Identity* Religious Life in the United States in Consecrated Life Today (UK St Paul Publications 1994) pp 17-4

Religious Life as Liminal

In recent years a number of models of religious life have been put forward. The one that makes most sense to me is that religious should be a liminal group in society. The concept of liminality was first introduced by Arnold Von Gennep in 1909. But Diarmuid O'Murchu[9] traces it back to Plato's Republic which envisaged a small but influential group whose task it was to live the deepest values of society, to be the guardians of its health and wholeness. The purpose of religious life is therefore to live and reflect back the deepest values of a society and culture.

If a society is undergoing rapid change this role is more significant and necessary than ever. We live in transitional times when little is clear. The danger is, that because the task is so demanding, religious simply fall into the cultural trap of keeping the system going. If, as Thomas Merton says, we concentrate on efficiency, then we put nearly all our energy into producing better schools, or better hospitals and trying to plug the increasing gaps. In other words we commit ourselves to work as hard, if not harder, than everyone else, we even produce our own religious workaholics. Throughout all this we try to keep smiling!

A busy culture doesn't need busy religious who simply reflect this imbalance. As liminal people we need to operate *within* as well as *without*. That also requires confronting some of our woundedness before we can heal the wounds of others. One critical way to address this, is to achieve a better integration of the outer and inner dimensions of our lives, to connect with a deeper sense of wholeness, because voices are increasingly being raised that our lives lack balance and harmony:

It is my belief that this ideal of universal harmony has been forfeited because of an almost exclusive concentration of the worth-whileness of the male point of view.[10]

We need to take a closer look at what this implies. It may be that our apparent decline in the measurable world of numbers and statistics may be offering religious life an opportunity which, if grasped, might purify our understanding of what is truly essential.

9 Diarmuid O'Murchu *Poverty Celibacy and Obedience*
   (N Y Crossroad Publishing Company 1999) p18

10 Pat Collins *Intimacy and the Hungers of the Heart*
   (Dublin The Columba Press 1992) p 144

CHAPTER TWO

The Two Journeys

It has become commonplace to speak of the spiritual life as a journey of faith. In reflection and reading on this theme for the retreats and courses I have given in recent years, I have come to see this journey in terms of a new balance or marriage between two archetypal aspects of our lives. Language is always a problem here, but it does seem helpful to present these two directions of the journey as the *outer* and the *inner*, the *without* and the *within*, or the *masculine* and the *feminine*. For a renewed religious life to speak to the culture of today, it seems that we must find a new balance between these two essential aspects of our lives.

In a sense the problem has always been recognised in the traditional division between contemplative and active religious orders. Whatever we say about the origins of religious life,[11] this distinction gradually became institutionalised, though there remained some congregations who combined both active and contemplative members. It is easy to see the contemplative life centred on prayer, work and reflection within a monastery or convent enclosure as rooted in the inner journey, the *within*. By contrast the active orders and congregations have manifested their charism in the form of a mission, such as nursing, teaching, or care of the poor, reflecting the outer journey, the *without*.

The Dualist Trap

One of the problems with this division is that it slotted all too easily into the kind of dualism, which has bedevilled our culture and thinking for centuries. It has effectively divided our world into categories such as spirit and matter, soul and body, sacred and profane, superior and inferior, good and evil, masculine and feminine. The problem with this way of thinking, alongside the divisions and splits that it created, were the value judgements that went with it. Spirit was considered better than matter, soul always more significant than body, masculine superior to feminine and so on. The splitting of light and dark also, as we shall see later, was not without its problems.

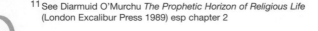

[11] See Diarmuid O'Murchu *The Prophetic Horizon of Religious Life*
(London Excalibur Press 1989) esp chapter 2

Our postmodern world is often criticised by religious believers for its deconstructive tendencies. Yet there are similarities with the work of the Old Testament prophets who were bravely critical of anything which did not reflect Yahweh's intentions for His people. The postmodern critique correctly identifies the injustice of excluding any group from full participation in society. Hence the evident concern to include all kinds of minorities, who have previously been overlooked by the dominant power, political or religious. This has helped to give impetus to a much healthier and more holistic spirituality which seeks to unify what had previously been divided.

From *either/or* to *both/and*

The Swiss Theologian, Hans Urs Von Balthazar, once asked in a lecture, "What is the most Catholic word?" I have used this question with many groups and received the usual answers: God, Jesus, Mary, the Pope etc. The answer supplied by Von Balthazar is the word AND. This is because a healthy spirituality must always be inclusive. It must embrace *both/and* in place of *either/or*. The answer to the old dualisms is to include both, in mutuality, not to see the differences in hierarchical terms.

A healthy spirituality therefore will be neither masculine nor feminine but androgynous, combining the two. If religious are is to be seen as a liminal group, addressing the deepest needs of our culture, then they need to find this new balance between the masculine and the feminine, the outer and the inner, the within and the without. I think there is some urgency in this task, because our world is clearly in transition at the moment. The values of modernity, of rationalism, of unbridled science and technology, of limitless progress, no longer fit the world we live in. We are not at ease with ourselves. The most worrying aspect of the current competitive patriarchal world-view is the ease with which it chooses violence as a solution to deep problems. Unless we address its underlying causes, the current threat of world terrorism will only increase if it is violently confronted. We need a new harmony, a new partnership between the dualities which have divided us. A different vision needs to emerge, which acknowledges the tensions at the heart of our lives and seeks not conquest or domination, but integration, mutuality, collaboration and wholeness.

The Heroic Journey

All of us are asked to undertake the hero/heroine's journey. This involves moving out from familiar surroundings and being tested with life's deepest experiences: love, pain, death, betrayal, courage and loyalty. The hero/heroine who has been wounded, bloodied and crucially transformed by these experiences, then returns home to share this wisdom with the community. It is interesting to note how many of our western mythical patterns, often demonstrated in films, frequently ignore this final phase as the hero rides off alone into the sunset. Like the male heroes of the Wild West, the contemporary James Bonds simply move off onto the next adventure.

Strangely, this weakness has been demonstrated by many hard-working religious, who do not know how to share their story. Their lives owe more to the stereotype of the rugged western heroes rather than the model of a Gospel community, trying to live the communal dream of the Kingdom. I feel that this has a lot do with our inability to accept the shadow side of our lives, to understand our woundedness and find ways of integrating it into our lives. In his study of archetypal myths, Joseph Campbell strongly emphasises this requirement of the hero at the end of his journey, to share the wisdom learned at such a high cost.[12]

Inner and Outer

We all begin life in the intimacy of our mother's womb. At our birth a profound bonding usually takes place which communicates the vital message that we are loved unconditionally. We are loved by our mother because of who we are, rather than anything we do. Our fathers also communicate this love, but in a slightly different way. We cannot stay in this Garden of Eden forever. I recall a conversation I had with a good friend of mine who is a teacher. When I asked her why she was looking so sad she spoke of her son, whom I had taught in school. He was leaving for college and she was upset. When I reminded her that he was 18 and needed to leave home she said she knew all that but, 'He is my baby!' I'm sure he would have been very embarrassed to hear his mother speak of him like that, but she was speaking at an archetypal level.

We all need to feel connected with home, with the world of simple being, of a deep belonging and union with our mother, but we cannot stay there.

12 Joseph Campbell *The Hero with a Thousand Faces* (N J Princeton University Press 1949)

It is usually the father's role to move us out into the world of doing, of activity. This is the world of work, in which we get valued more by what we do and achieve. It is the world of thinking, of reason and analysis. It is the world of science and technology and it has clearly transformed our lives in all kinds of ways. It is the outer or masculine journey. This is especially significant for males, who need to feel the approval of another male figure. Our mother's love is natural and unconditional; the love of our father, in a sense, has to be earned and carries a different yet vital significance. Daughters also need this approval from their fathers, but it is especially significant for boys.

This outer journey also places us in touch with the condition of others; ours is an unequal world and many in our world suffer from deprivations and various kinds of poverty. It gives our story a deeper meaning and value when we discover how we are connected to the stories of others. The journey then begins to take on heroic form, as men and women struggle to build a world of greater justice and human dignity. Virtually every apostolic religious order or congregation was founded with this in mind. In response to the appeal of the Church at Vatican II this has also been a key element in all programmes of religious renewal. Concern for the poor and the needy reflects this attempt to take the Gospel seriously, and religious have shown great courage and dedication in responding to this challenge.

The journey *without* is the way of separation and encounter. It is the place of critical reflection and analysis, leading to judgements and confrontation. The Gospel obliges us to read history and the signs of the times from the perspective of the poor. This will put us in conflict with those forces who see religion and spirituality as a kind of palliative, a comforting place to withdraw from the struggles of politics and economics. When men and women engage with this aspect of the journey they are tapping into those vital masculine energies that engage the dragons and demons of this world with fortitude and courage. It is a dangerous adventure and many today find it too challenging and prefer to spend their lives in what has been called the *soft feminine*, a cosy world which refuses to engage in the difficult and self-sacrificing call to create a more just world. This soft world is a great temptation and it is one that the Church and religious life have fallen into, by a distorted Marian piety, which does scant service to the woman who, more than any other disciple, knew how to integrate all aspects of her personality. This is a task for all of us, men and women together. Some women religious have taken this challenge up in recent years with enormous courage. It isn't just a male thing. It is always a case of *both/and* rather than *either/or*.

Right and Left Brain

This need for mutuality and integration has been further reinforced by some research findings of recent years. In 1981 Robert Sperry won the Nobel Prize for his work in revealing that the brain is divided into two hemispheres, right and left. What is interesting is that they both know reality in different ways. This fact helps us to understand one of the fundamental problems at the heart of western spirituality today. Its effects can be seen in so many ways, not least in the way that religious life is currently being lived. This goes deeper than whether people are judged conservative or liberal. It affects how we see and understand reality, and spirituality is primarily about seeing. It also touches on one of the core problems in active religious life, the difficulty that many religious have with prayer life. We have all been taught that prayer is primarily about thinking, and as long as we believe that, we will be caught in the left-brain trap.

The culture we live in demands that we spend most of our time in the left brain. The left brain promotes order, clarity, rationality, analysis and control. Those who were comfortable in this mode of operating usually were rewarded with promotion in the Church. It isn't easy to survive religious life if you are right-brained. The right hemisphere of the brain is where the creative, intuitive and feeling functions are located.

Anyone with artistic, poetic, or imaginative leanings was usually regarded with some suspicion. Left-brain people believe that if you want to understand reality you have to take it apart, through analysis. Many Religious Chapters operate on the methodology that splits a theme into parts which are discussed separately and then put together with a cut and paste job at the end. By contrast right-brain people look at the whole. Clearly both ways of looking are necessary for a full understanding; here as elsewhere it has to be *both/and* and not *either/or*. We need the left and the right brain to understand fully; we need to combine the within and the without.

Our western civilisation has long been locked into the *either/or* mentality. In the Catholic Church we have put so much energy into dogma, doctrines and structures, with rules and regulations. We love to create winners and losers; we have become good at excluding. In the Gospels, it seems that Jesus demonstrated table-fellowship in the most inclusive manner; in the history of the Church we seem to have used the Eucharist to divide and exclude. In my own experience I have seen too many elderly people whose religious lives are controlled by fears of getting it wrong, whether it is missing Mass on Sunday, or for so many priests, failing to navigate the intricacies of the Daily Office or the liturgical Ordo. This is all left-brain material, and because it was passed on to us in an unbalanced way it has left us trapped, and deprived us of the freedom of the sons and daughters of God, about which St Paul was so eloquent.

A New Balance

In the dualistic environment, we have long inhabited, it might be thought that all we have to do in our spiritual journeys would be to move from putting our energy and focus from the outer journey back into the inner one. This would be a grave mistake. What we have to do is find the proper balance. Some commentators argue that, for the first thousand years of its history, the Church was primarily right-brained. In the last thousand years there can be no doubt that the emphasis has been on the left brain. We have sought control and manipulation of people's lives. We have overdosed on rules and regulations. The sacramental world of symbolism, which is clearly right-brained, has been forced into the logical rational boxes of legitimacy and validity.

One of the consequences of this imbalance has been that even the work of renewal in religious life has often been hijacked by the predominance of the outer journey. This was almost inevitable given the kind of culture in which we live. As Nygren and Ukeritis[13] make clear, religious have been largely unaware of the cultural influences on our spirituality. All the emphasis in our culture today is on doing, on performance, on programmes, on targets, on what can be measured.

If we ask the question, "Why religious life?" Surely it cannot be reduced to providing a better, more dedicated, harder working labour force. I am not saying that doing is not important, that would be to fall into the old dualistic trap of *either/or*. But in moving to a *both/and* spirituality we need to redress the balance. If we are to be liminal people we have to address the deepest

[13] *Transforming Tradition* 1994

hungers of our age, not simply feed into its obsessions. The world today seems quite capable of producing good teachers and nurses. Again I am not saying that religious cannot be good teachers or nurses. But what I am saying is that if that is all we are then it does provoke the question, "Why religious life?"

In all the uncertainties of a postmodern world one thing does seem to be emerging. Despite all the apparent superficiality of a media-driven culture, and its obsessions with materialism, the cult of celebrity, with individualism, and moral relativism, there exists at a discernable level a new hunger for meaning. The search for meaning is, at heart, a spiritual quest. In a busy extraverted outer-directed culture there is a real need for some people who can step back from the whirlwind of activity and rediscover the inner journey, to begin to explore what the Chief Rabbi, Jonathon Sacks, calls:
the inner landscape of the human spirit.[14]

Religious alone do not make this journey. Essentially it is the human journey: it is the call to explore the very mystery of who we are, and to discover that God is not an object who exists *out there*. God is a deeply personal presence that we discover in the very heart of our being. We are called to be heroes and heroines in our own story.

The Wisdom Figure

In the journeys and stories recorded in the great literature and dramas of mankind, there is often a need for a wise protector, a figure of wisdom, who will offer the pilgrim some advice and help on his or her way. These wisdom figures may be rare; but what a blessing they bring. If societies do require liminal groups who are in touch with their deepest values, could it not be argued that religious life is one of the institutionalised forms of such a group? To make the claim is not to guarantee that every religious will make that journey; I am simply suggesting that religious life should be able to provide structures and conditions to make it possible and favourable.

In this way religious life could bring some greater harmony and balance to the masculine and the feminine journey. Instead of simply seeing a renewed religious life as providing a more efficient labour force for the Church, it could be seen as creating structures that would give space and leisure for the essential human task of integrating the *inner* and the outer, the *within* and the *without*. I am conscious that the use of words such as space and

---

[14] Jonathon Sacks *The Dignity of Difference* (London Continuum 2002) p 5

leisure can create resistance. I think that it is inevitable because we are all much more comfortable operating as left-brain people. Words like space and leisure bring on the all too familiar guilt feelings in many religious.

There is also the feeling that somehow this inner journey is a kind of soft option. One often hears religious, usually male, speaking with pride about *working at the coal face*. Maybe we need to show similar energy in working at our own inner coal face. There can be no doubt that this is a very demanding task and it probably explains why so few people attempt it. We need to excavate our own souls if we are to be able to offer any guidance or help to anyone else. The pathfinder needs to have walked the path. More than anything else the guide needs to have been wounded, to have failed, to have experienced brokeness and imperfection.

A Journey of Soul

If a renewed religious life is to offer any hope for the future, and that is what it is called to offer, especially to the young, then we need to make a journey of soul, the journey within. Perhaps we have been too easily seduced by a narrow understanding of spiritual journey, one which bypassed our essential humanity. We sought perfection in an almost angelic-like existence. So many of our problems with sexuality are caught up here. We need to re-discover the truth of the incarnation, of a God who became fully and totally human. As we re-find our humanity we will re-discover our souls. This is no easy task; it can be very daunting.

There are those who argue that all the great explorations of our planet are now over. At the beginning of this millennium many people expressed the view that the most significant moment in the twentieth century was the landing on the moon in 1969. It was a truly extraordinary achievement of the journey without, science and technology at its very best and most inspiring, a triumph of the human spirit which has always striven to reach beyond the stars. As we begin the 21st century we are faced by a new challenge, perhaps an even more daunting one, but at the same time one that calls us to a place we have always wanted to be. It is to take up Joseph Campbell's forgotten dimension of the hero's and heroine's journey:[15] it is nothing other than the journey home, because when we make both journeys the two become one. The hero/heroine returns home wounded but wiser; that is the gift of a fully human spirituality.

---

15 *The Hero with a Thousand Faces*

CHAPTER THREE

The Future is Relational

Bill Clinton and his political advisers famously summed up their successful campaign to oust President George Bush Snr in the succinct phrase: 'It's the economy, stupid!' If we want to discern the future direction for religious life it can all be summed up in the word *relational*. It is the contention of this book that religious life has to re-discover its role as a liminal force in society. The problem is that we are living through a period of such profound transition that it is difficult to keep abreast of everything that is happening. Given the contemporary cultural bias towards action and the outer journey, it makes it all the more important and indeed prophetic, that some people step off the merry-go-round and begin to ask deeper questions. In many ways our times can be summed up in the story of the farmer, looking over a hedge, who sees a man clattering towards him on horseback at great speed. As he passes him he asks the rider where he's heading. 'No idea', shouts the man, as he sweeps by, 'Ask the horse!'

In our Catholic tradition Mary has always been presented to us as the model for all spirituality. The irony is that the focus has nearly always been on the inner qualities of Mary and her quiet unassuming feminine virtues to the detriment of the strongly masculine side of her spirituality, as evidenced in the Magnificat, with its strong proclamation of a new order. But let us consider her feminine gift of reflection; her ability to reflect, ponder and store things up in her heart. It is in that maternal climate that Luke describes Jesus as increasing in wisdom and stature before God and men.[16] It is this reflective quality that increasingly needs to be brought to bear on our workaholic culture. I stress again that action is not a bad thing, clearly it is essential in apostolic religious life, but it does need to be balanced with a deeper and healthier energy. In a forward to a book by Barbara Fiand, Joan Chittister suggests the crucial nature of this inner work for the world in which we are living:

> **To lead an efficient, distanced, and almost frenetic society from fascination with action to concern for meanings could well be the final gift of the Church to this time. Without it we may certainly perish in both soul and body at the hands of the systems we have made.[17]**

---

[16] Luke 2:51-52

[17] *Releasement* (N Y: Crossroad 1987) p ix

The Search for Wholeness

To do this we need to have a clearer understanding of this transitional period of history in which we find ourselves. The drawback of Vatican II's famous turning to embrace the modern world is that it coincided with the world beginning to shake off the inadequacies of modernity. While postmodernity is still too close to us to be fully evaluated, it seems clear that it feels keenly the poverty of technological reason and scientific *progress* which continues to damage the ecology of the planet. The split between objectivity and subjectivity is further seen as damaging to the ecology of soul and spirit. It is this discontent that offers hope to those who would see signs of a spiritual revival in this new emergent culture.

While at one level there has been an increase in fragmentation, in dispersal, in loneliness, in the collapse of all total explanations whether Marxist, Capitalist, or Christian, there is nevertheless a discernible interest in the relational, in the value of community. The recent phenomenon of *Reality TV* has seen the remarkable success of programmes like *Big Brother* and *Celebrity Big Brother* which tap into this hunger for relationships. Cultural commentators such as Michael Paul Gallagher are led to the view that such interest demonstrates that:

> **Spirituality becomes not just a fashionable term but a real issue in this era beyond the oppressions of modernity.**[18]

The linking of spirituality with the relational is at the heart of a contemporary reading of the signs of the times. Any renewal programme which ignores this is doomed to failure. The relational paradigm shift is strongly apparent in so many other disciplines today. It seeks to include rather than exclude; to connect rather than fragment, to address intimacy needs rather than simply work-related goals. An integrated spirituality suggests that here also the *both/and* approach offers the potential of the deepest human growth. Our search within will lead to a more human journey without.

While commentators differ in assessing the length of the dominance of the patriarchal age, there is genuine agreement that in the last hundred years or so, women have begun to claim some kind of equality. Sebastian Moore expresses this forcefully:

> **Now the game is up, the patriarchal age is everywhere in crisis**

---

18 Michael Paul Gallagher *Clashing Symbols* (Darton Longman & Todd 1997) p93

and indeed threatening us with extinction, and there is beginning the woman's quest for her identity, a quest of comparable magnitude with the male quest that has shaped three millennia.[19]

One of the means of restoring the feminine inner dimension to all our lives, female and male, is to explore the area of story, of symbolism, of literature. The world of myth is another rich seam which is helping us to recover a sense of wholeness. In Chapter Four, I shall consider how this can help us to understand what is happening to religious life. What I want to examine first are some of the interesting developments in the world of theology which have implications for the recovery of a liminal vision of religious life. In the Gospels we hear how Jesus answers the question:

Master, what is the greatest commandment in the Law?[20]

The evangelist notes that, as on so many other occasions, the Pharisees and the Sadducees were not honestly seeking the truth; they asked the question to disconcert Jesus. The powerful answer Jesus gives is to say that:

You must love the Lord your God with all your heart, with all your soul and with all your mind. This is the greatest and the first commandment. The second resembles it: you must love your neighbour as yourself. On these two commandments hang the whole Law and the Prophets also.[21]

There is no doubt that, for Jesus, the commandment to love God takes priority. It is the first and greatest commandment. The second clearly flows from it and is intimately connected: love of neighbour and love of self, the part which has often been misunderstood. What cannot be in any doubt is that it is profoundly relational. For Jesus, what comes first and foremost is the heart. Next he mentions the soul and then the mind. Here we have a wonderfully balanced theology and spirituality that integrates heart, soul and mind.

The Shift from the Calculative Mind

If we look at the history of the Church, however, I think we would have to admit that we haven't always got this balance right. The emphasis has long been on the calculative mind, the rational mind, that seeks to analyse, to

[19] Sebastian Moore *The Inner Loneliness* (London Darton Longman &Todd 1982) p 73

[20] Matthew 22: 35

[21] Matthew 22:37-40

distinguish, to separate and judge. These are all necessary tasks, but if they are unduly divorced from the heart, then theology gets locked into an overly masculine style, and it easily becomes judgmental and exclusive. We have a long history of playing the game of theological winners and losers as we identify lists of heresies.

It is no surprise that the word *dogma* has become deeply unpopular today. We split reality into parts and rarely put them together as a whole. Once again the *without* dominates the *within*. The words of Jesus make it clear that the heart must precede the mind in our response to God. The search for a more collaborative and less divisive view of truth and of reality is beginning to grow.

What is truly fascinating today is that even science is moving in this direction. Scientists are discovering that reality is not so easy to pin down and analyse as was once thought. When you examine the smallest realities, atomic particles, and the huge realities of galaxies and black holes, it's all mystery. We are not after all in charge. Some say that the best scientists today are having to become mystics, and the thinking religious are becoming much more aware of psychology, both trying to come to terms with the non-rational. We are re-learning a sense of humility, awe and wonder; appreciating the mysterious nature of all reality, especially the human person.

This development is helping us to recover a truly holistic understanding of the world. One that helps us to understand better the God of Jesus, the gifts of creation, the blessedness of everything, and the need to respect diversity within a greater unity. We are learning, in other words, to see. I would go even further and say that we are learning to see with the eyes of God. All the great religions share a common understanding that spirituality is about the cleansing of vision, of learning to see what is truly real. Catholic religious life with its rich variety of charisms is one aspect of the endless diversity of approaches to the divine. We are not the only pebbles on the beach. All the religious traditions, Hinduism, Judaism, Islam, Sikhism and Buddhism, have produced their own liminal groupings.[22]

---

22 Diarmuid O'Murchu *The Prophetic Horizon of Religious Life* See Chapter 1

The Contemplative Mind

It has been suggested that the eastern tradition has kept the contemplative mystical dimension alive better than the West. On the other hand the western forms of religious life have been stronger in the active and prophetic role. Here, as elsewhere, we see the baleful effects of dualistic thinking which separates sacred from secular, doing from being, mission from contemplation, the outer from the inner. What matters in the postmodern world, is that these divisions have to be healed if religious life, in whatever form it may take in the future, is to address the deepest hungers.

My argument in this book is that an over dominant patriarchal, masculine way of doing and living is at the root of our cultural, and therefore spiritual, crisis today. The need is not to replace it with an over dominant feminine way of life. It is to seek a new and harmonious relationship between the two. This is the challenge of the twenty first century. For this to happen we have to make the inner journey both as individuals and as groups, if this healing is to occur. This is not an easy journey, no heroic journey ever is, and it is a particular challenge for apostolic orders because of the stress and emphasis on mission. This drive can never be taken away but it has to be seen as serving the heart of the central quest and purpose of religious life, which is nothing other than the search for God:

> **Religious life, the vowed life, is an expression of the biblical call to holiness; it is a public enactment of an ancient quest; the quest to respond to the God who has already touched us and haunted us. It is no less than the quest for holiness.**[23]

This quest lies at the heart of all human experience, all longing, all desire. At periods of history it may well lie dormant. In fact, in the opinion of many wise people today, our busy work-oriented culture is stifling and deadening this very desire and search. But it cannot go away; if it did we would cease to be human because it contains the seeds of our very identity as creatures made in the image and likeness of God. The purpose of our lives finds fulfilment in that quest, that heroic journey which, as T S Eliot reminds us, brings us back to where we started, but with a new understanding and vision. It was this insight that led Carl Jung to suggest that the problem of every patient who came to him in the second half of life, was at root a religious problem.

[23] Donald Senior *Biblical Foundations for Religious Life* in *Living in the Meantime* (N J Mahwah Paulist Press ed Paul Philibert 1994) p 58

When we make the inner journey to the true centre of our being and discover God in the sacred space of the heart, we do not move away from our neighbour; in fact we move closer because all reality is held in God's loving power. To suggest otherwise is to fall victim to the old dualism which has been found incomplete and wanting. In the Gospel, Jesus doesn't just link love of God and love of neighbour, he identifies them as the same. Whatever we do to the least is done to Him:

for I was hungry .. I was thirsty .. I was a stranger .. I was sick .. I was in prison.[24]

The Convergence of Theology and Spirituality

One of the most encouraging developments in the Church in recent years has been the re-connecting of theology with spirituality. The recovery of the central importance of the doctrine of the Trinity, as a relational not an abstract doctrine, has been at the heart of this process. The primary model for understanding the Church today is *communion*; the primary model for understanding spirituality is *relational*. This has profound consequences for a renewed understanding of religious life, and demands a major shift of focus from a functional model to a relational one.

In the early centuries of the Church there was always a clear unity between theology and spirituality, between knowledge and wisdom, between academic thought and contemplation, or between theory and practice if you want to put it simply. Patristic theology certainly reflected this unity as did the golden age of monastic theology in the West, which stretched from Gregory the Great in the 6th century through Anselm of Canterbury in the 11th to Bernard of Clairvaux in the 12th century. It is difficult to be precise but it was around this time that a change of direction occurred, and under men like Peter Abelard theology became divorced from the monasteries, and academic schools were set up.

Theology then began to develop increasingly as a speculative enterprise. It was taking place in the head; it became a left-brain exercise. The discipline of the mind was separated from the spiritual or devotional life. There were always exceptions to this trend such as Bonaventure or Aquinas but even Aquinas ended up reducing what we would today call spirituality, to a sub-category of moral theology and quite separate from dogma:

---

[24] Matthew 24:31-46

The split between theology and spirituality was really a tragedy for both. Its intellectual origins lie in the theological developments in the High Middle Ages where 'thinking' began to be understood as a mastery of facts and details rather than attention to the truth expressed in symbols. To put it more simply, reason began to triumph over imagination and the ability to define truth over experiences of the sacred.[25]

The Reformation and the Counter-Reformation only increased this split. We have ended up with a serious division between the Church's head and the Church's heart. Until we can get out of our heads and into our hearts, or into our feminine soul, then we will not be able to give birth to Christ in our world. A healthy image of God must lie at the heart of the renewal process.

Religious Life as the Quest for God

If religious life is an adventure into the love of God, then how do we understand God? More precisely how does God relate to us? How, therefore, should we relate to each other, both in community and with those with whom we work? Here contemporary theologians are recovering a much richer understanding of the doctrine of the Trinity, one that sees it in relational terms:

Revelation is once again seen as the amazing love-story of God's desire to be intimately among us in human form. Full of intense compassion, God wished to create out of pure love, and then, in time, to become that creation. That becoming happened in Jesus Christ. In him it was revealed that God's heart beats in all our hearts, that all our bodies are temples of the Holy Spirit, that every creature is a divine work of art.[26]

The whole mission of Jesus was aimed at revealing to us good news of how God is intimately joined to the human heart through love. He wanted to restore to Israel a religion of the heart:

**If anyone loves me he will keep my word, and my Father will love him, and we shall come to him and make our home with him...
I have said these things to you while still with you; but the advocate, the Holy Spirit whom the Father will send in my name will teach you everything and remind you of all I have said to you.[27]**

25 Philip Sheldrake *Spirituality and Theology* (London Darton Longman & Todd 1998) p 40

26 Daniel J O'Leary *Passion for the Possible* (Dublin The Columba Press 2000) p 16

27 John 14:23; 25-26

It's all relational. Our God is not distant and unmoved. He comes to us in Jesus, one who shares our weaknesses and limitations. He expresses His solidarity with us, not in taking away the pain and mystery of life, but by passionately embracing that mystery. He calls us into a community in which we can bear each other's burdens. The God of Father, Son and Holy Spirit invites us to share in the divine life of love and communion.

In the time when theology was divorced from spirituality the doctrine of the Trinity was reduced to a kind of sacred mathematics. In recent years the Church has deepened her reflection and understanding of a God of love, who shares life with humanity in inter-personal love that leads to communion and mutuality. A spirituality that is divorced from theology often encouraged an individualistic piety, and there is still plenty of evidence of this in religious life. The recent stress in Church documents on religious life, expressed in Chapters, has been to place the person in the context of a healthy community life and mission.

Theology of Communion and Relational Spirituality

In recent times there have been three key documents on the three great vocations in the Church. In 1988 we had the publication of **Christifidelis Laici**, on the new understanding of the laity in the Church. In 1992 we had the document on the priesthood, **Pastores Dabo Vobis**, in 1996 **Vita Consecrata**, on the religious life. All these documents are rooted in the theology of communion and lead naturally into a relational spirituality. Studies on Vatican II have concluded that the ecclesiology of communion is the underlying vision.

In **Vita Consecrata**, the same underlying theology and spirituality is evident. Pope John Paul II has a whole section (n 17-22) on the relationship between religious life and the Trinity. He describes the vows as particular gifts of the Trinity:

> **The deepest meaning of the evangelical counsels is revealed when they are viewed in relation to the Holy Trinity, the source of holiness. They are in fact an expression of the love of the Son for the Father in the unity of the Holy Spirit.**[28]

The Pope goes on to say that religious life, throughout its history, has always had the task of keeping alive in the Church the obligation of

28   *Vita Consecrata* (Rome Vatican Press 1996) n 21

fraternity and communion as a form of witness to the Trinity. It is the re-emergence of this insight which is the driving energy behind so much of the collaborative initiatives and language that has dominated recent Chapters of many Orders and Congregations. The Pope even goes on to say that if we can live from this theological perspective, then our lives will demonstrate that sharing in communion with the Trinity can change human relationships.

It is this vision of a theology of communion and a relational spirituality that promises a way forward in this time of transition. It finds echoes in a new awareness of the need to marry the independence and excessive individualism of recent years with a new sense of community, of a common mission shared. Yet problems remain. For some time now, the Church and Religious Congregations have been producing fine documents yet very few of them seem to inspire deep change. If it is all about relationships then we have to find ways of connecting the beautiful statements with the human heart and the human person in all our emotional fragility and brokeness. A journey into the heart is called for:

You cannot reach people if you are divorced from your own emotions.[29]

For this to happen the hero/heroine has to make the journey within. It is necessary to engage our deepest selves, and to confront what we find there with trust, with honesty, with some tears and a lot of humility.

---

[29] Dorothee Solle *The Strength of the Weak* (London Westminster Press 1984) p 84

CHAPTER FOUR

The Connecting Story

While confidently rejecting the rather shallow myth of endless progress, which held modernity together, the postmodern world is less confident about any kind of vision that lays claim to our lives. Postmodernism knows what it is against; it is much less sure what it is for. By restricting meaning into the straightjacket of science and technology, modernity paved the way for its failure to deliver happiness. Postmodernism remains deeply pessimistic and sceptical about any pattern or meaning to life. It has created a society close at times to nihilism, which is quick to discredit and apportion blame for its disappointments.

So, we are left with the private self, who alone cannot bear the pain and the mystery of life. In its public face postmodern society manifests increasing signs of depression, of rising and often violent crime, of drugs, of trivialised sex, abortions and increasing alcoholism among the young. To fill the emptiness of our lives we are offered the new religion of consumerism.

As I drive south along the M60 motorway, the Manchester Ring Road, I pass one of the great symbols of our age. It is a large shopping mall known as the Trafford Centre. I don't know what the architects of this imposing structure had in mind, but with its two large domes and several statues, it clearly resembles a cathedral. For many today shopping has almost become a religion. Lines of vehicles can be seen, every weekend, as *worshippers* approach the sanctuary of consumerism. Descartes' maxim, 'I think therefore I am,' has been replaced by 'I shop therefore I am.' This *religion* of the postmodern world is centred on the maximising of choice: more styles, more clothes, more electronic goods, more television channels, and the constant promotion of the latest *must have* item.

These things are harmless in themselves. In a way they reflect the success story of western civilisation. We all rely on improved medical technology, on a variety of labour-saving devices, on greater mobility, the internet, e-mail and mobile phones. However, the amazing success of the scientific and technological revolution of recent centuries, the ever-increasing exploration of the *outer journey* has not been without its price. The cost has been to our *inner world* and its effects are pervasive:

> **Our western heroic achievements are the envy of the rest of the world, but they were won at the cost of our capacity for warmth, feeling, contentment and serenity. We are so rich in things and so poor in feminine values.**[30]

The problem is experienced primarily at the relational level. It touches on the issue of values. It suggests a serious imbalance, which is affecting our ability to connect with each other at a profound level. Moreover, we don't really know what to do with this pain. Discussions on television, and radio phone-in programmes reflect a high level of hurt and anger. Shopping is regularly described as *retail therapy*, mainly for women. We rarely ask why this therapy is constantly needed. The shopping addiction seems to be a way of avoiding our relational wounds. The irony is that it is the masculine, patriarchal culture of economic competition and success that has produced this problem. Retail therapy is the shadow side of the commodity life-style.

Relational Woundedness

I recall watching a television programme in the UK, which debated the performance of the government of the day, in regard to its promises to improve the lot of the poor. Everyone present in the studio was there presumably because of their concern for their neighbour, for genuinely altruistic motives. Despite this the programme led to some very animated and angry exchanges; in fact the word *venomous* would best describe the atmosphere in that studio. Lest we religious feel ourselves superior to this kind of nastiness we need to ask ourselves why there is often so much anger within religious communities. I remember the startling words of a Benedictine retreat preacher who expressed the view that, in his experience, many religious communities seem to be run on aggression.

What I want to do in this chapter is to explore further the roots of our relational woundedness. If religious life is meant to model a relational spirituality, then we need to explore this issue at greater depth. Too many

---

[30] Robert A Johnson Femininity *Lost and Regained* (N Y Harper Perennial 1990) p 6

renewal documents deal with religious life at the level of the ideal. Authentic spirituality has to deal with what is real.

Left-brain analytical thinking alone cannot deal with these matters in any depth. The outer world is the world of competition, of achievement, of market forces that drive this whole system of buying and selling and it will always value things over people. This system which has produced so much success, at the level of material possessions and things, has got so out of balance that it will actively resist attempts to redress it. In the western world the icons of our culture are celebrities, people who are at the top of the system, famous for being famous, whose lives are held up for our admiration, for their outer appearance, their looks, and their clothes, their image. They are presented to us as the people *who have it all*, the ones who have made it, the people we are supposed to envy.

This might appear harmless enough, but at a deeper level it diminishes and devalues the sense of our own value and self-worth. In projecting our fantasy life onto the rich and famous we kill the hero/heroine within ourselves. The liminal task for religious is not to proclaim that we are any better than anyone else. It is to have the courage in this postmodern world to make the heroic journey within. It is to offer healing and wisdom. Such heroism demands great courage, trust and honesty, and not everyone wishes to pay that price, especially when our culture is so clever at entertaining us with so much superficiality.

From Outer to Inner

As the last century came to an end a number of surveys asked people to identify the most significant event of the twentieth century. Most people chose the landing on the moon by astronauts in 1969. It was a truly inspiring event, but in almost every sense it summed up the achievement of a technically brilliant outer-directed society. What better symbol could you have of the *outer journey* as mankind finally landed on the moon? As we begin the twenty first century, however, a different kind of heroism is needed, equally daring: we need to go within.

If our postmodern culture is to be saved or redeemed today it needs heroes and heroines, people who will not be afraid to make the journey to confront their deepest and truest selves. We have to learn how to re-connect with our spiritual selves; we have to go deep into our hearts, to make what the poet Christopher Fry calls:

The longest stride known to man.[31]

To go within, we have to enter the world of story, of myth, of the symbolic, of reflection and active imagination.[32] It requires a re-connection to the Sacred Feminine, but it needs to be made by both men and women. Women may well lead this journey but it needs to be made by men also so that we can achieve the sacred marriage between masculine and feminine and bring true healing to our world. Otherwise we will be back in the world of *either/or* dualism. The rise of feminism was undoubtedly one of the real signs of the times in the twentieth century. Women had to struggle to gain access to the masculine world of work and achievement. Having arrived there some women are discovering its inner emptiness: its relational poverty. Many of us lack a genuine intimacy, with ourselves, with others, and with God.

The way back is to move out of the strictures of purely left-brain, linear, objective thinking and to enter the inner world of the unconscious that can only be accessed through intuition and dream images, through the symbolic, through story. Such stories lead into paradox and mystery. So much of the ministry of Jesus is taken up with these kinds of stories, with parables that invite us to enter the mystery with the eyes of a child, with a sense of wonder and awe. Just consider how rarely he answers questions directly, and yet we have put so much energy into providing answers for people's heads!

The Need for Myth

Great cultures have always attempted to shape and give sense to life through great stories. While factual data and analysis keeps us at a detached distance, stories invite us in to their world of meaning. Great drama, literature and poetry have always done this. Mythical stories are perhaps the most necessary because they deal with truth at its deepest and most archetypal. Myths more than any other form of story telling appeal to the latent hero and heroine in us all.

---

31 *A Sleep of Prisoners*

32 For practical exercises in the inner journey I would recommend Peter Hannon *The Search for Something More* (Dublin The Columba Press 2001)

Two of the great mythical stories that have been receiving renewed attention in our times are the story of the fisher king which is part of the myth of the Holy Grail, the chalice said to have been used by Jesus at the Last Supper,[33] and the story of the handless maiden. Both these stories touch on the wounded feeling function in our culture, the result of over dominance of the masculine *objective* way of thinking. The fisher king story maps the journey from the masculine to the inner feminine; the handless maiden looks at the wound from a feminine perspective. Since all of us, men and women, are locked into the prevailing masculine consciousness today, the resistance to this kind of journey is strong. After all we all have so many things to do. It is no exaggeration to say that a commitment to explore such matters does require a real degree of heroism. All the great religions share a common aim in trying to get us to see reality differently:

The masculine elements are particularly hostile to any change in consciousness. It has been said that Jesus had no trouble with the women near him but came to grief with the prevailing masculine law and order of his time.[34]

The Story of the Fisher King

According to legend the Grail was the chalice used by Jesus at the Last Supper. It was kept by a fisher king who is unaware of its significance. He is unwell, almost bent-double in pain, relieved only by the activity of fishing. The whole kingdom shares his sickness and no one can bring healing.

A young knight, Parsival, is given three rules to live by. He must neither seduce nor be seduced and he must seek the Holy Grail. When he finds it he must ask the question: 'Whom does the Grail serve?' After many adventures he comes across a richly attired man, bent double in pain, fishing in the lake. The man advises him where he can shelter and stay the night in a nearby castle.

That night in the castle Parsival discovers that the man he met is in fact the king. In a magical procession the Grail is carried into the chamber. Parsival is so astonished at everything that is happening that he fails to ask the question, 'Whom does the Grail serve?' As a result the king is not healed, nor is his land, and he is carried from the room still in pain. The next

---

33 See the following for fuller treatment Robert A Johnson *The Fisher King and the Handless Maiden* (Harper San Francisco 1993) Johnson considers the story from the wider cultural perspective. For a more specific reference to implications for religious life see Barbara Fiand *Wrestling with God* (N Y: Crossroad Publishing Company 1996). Richard Rohr examines the Grail legend from the perspective of masculine spirituality in Richard Rohr *Quest for the Grail* (N Y: Crossroad Publishing company 1997) and Peter Hannon *Follow Your Dream* (Dublin: The Columba Press 1998 pp 66-70) considers its application to human sinfulness.

34 Robert A Johnson *Femininity Lost and Regained* p 32

morning Parsival finds an empty castle. He mounts his horse and rides off and the castle disappears.

This story addresses the wounded-feeling faculty in all of us. As a young energetic knight Parsival is a powerful symbol of the masculine need to go out and engage the world. It is a necessary journey. None of us can stay in the warm and cosy atmosphere of the maternal feminine. He is so fascinated, however, with all the action that comes his way that he loses his awareness. When the crucial moment arrives to ask the question he is supposed to ask, a question aimed at discovering true meaning, he misses the opportunity. As a result neither the king nor his realm receive the healing they need. The image of the king fishing in the lake illustrates the need to connect with water, the great symbol of unconscious life. At the beginning of his active ministry Jesus fully immersed himself into the waters of the Jordan. As an ancient story, the Grail Myth has many versions, but it is generally agreed that the king is wounded in the male, generative part of a man's being. This wound demonstrates the wounded-feeling function. This is not just about emotion: the feeling function is our capacity to value or give worth and significance.

Woundedness manifests itself in the lack of balance in our lives. Like Parsival we are so caught up in an endless round of activities that we lose touch with our feeling capacity. These activities are not in themselves bad, many of them may be in the service of mission, but they do drain our energy and leave little time or enthusiasm for the journey within. We then begin to build walls around this inner sanctuary, the inner castle of our souls. There are too many dragons to be slain and we fail to connect with the unconscious. We become infected with postmodern shallowness. We may be very hard workers but we never stop to ask the question: 'Whom does the Grail serve? What is it all for?' As the man on the speeding horse said in reply to the inquiry where he was heading: 'Ask the horse!' We have lost our sense of what is truly valuable and significant for our health and wholeness:

It is eloquent that the slang expression for a sophisticated person is 'cool'. We may die of our 'coolness', which is one of the characteristics of the fisher king-wounded man.[35]

---

35 Robert A Johnson *The Fisher King and the Handless Maiden* p 17

Our culture values reason, logic and objectivity over affection, intuition and subjectivity. It prefers order and clarity over paradox and mystery. In the Church and religious life we have sought the spirit of perfection, we promote workaholics, we are all so busy doing so many things. In society we pay the price of valuing things before people. Men and women, work long and hard to provide more material things for their families. Little energy is left for the task of relating within these families. Family life continues to fragment, and the children pay the price.

The Wounds of Religious Life

In religious life, while we dedicate ourselves to our respective missions and continue to produce our idealised documents and statements, we pay the price of being unable to relate both within and without our communities. We lack the ability to be truly intimate with others by avoiding the demands of community. We hold back from true intimacy with God as prayer life goes on the back burner and we lack the ability to be intimate with ourselves as we neglect the inner journey of the soul.

The beauty of myths is that they work at many different levels of meaning. While Robert A Johnson applies this story to the wounded-feeling function at the heart of our western culture, Barbara Fiand sees it as a parable for religious life in our times. This is a particular problem for apostolic religious who have to operate in this busy extraverted culture. But for religious to maintain their liminal purpose the balance has to be re-dressed. We need to re-connect with our souls, to face our woundedness, to embrace our brokeness. We need to connect the *outer Parsival* with the *inner fisher king* to heal our dislocated lives. The word *symbolic* means to unite; we need to re-connect our story, the within and the without of our lives.

Will it be male or female religious who lead us into this inner wisdom? The journey is not the same for both. To be male involves the integration of the feminine into the masculine; to be female involves the integration of the masculine journey into the feminine. I have argued that all of us today tend to operate in the outer masculine competitive world. The challenge for women is that in having at long last entered this world they do not sacrifice their inner feminine core. A look at another mythical story helps to reveal what is at stake. This story deals more with the feminine journey.

The Handless Maiden

A miller, who works hard and long, makes a bargain with the devil, who offers, for a fee, to increase his output and decrease his labour. What he doesn't realise is that the devil is speaking about his daughter. She manages to avoid Satan's clutches but at the cost of her hands which the devil cuts off. In exile she meets a young king; they fall in love and marry and he fashions for her a pair of silver hands. She bears a child and they live happily until the king has to leave on a long journey. Here the devil intervenes again and interrupts letters between the couple. In great desolation the woman is exiled again until she meets an angel who leads her deep into the forest and into a house with the inscription: 'All who enter here shall be free'. After living here deep in the forest for seven years her natural hands grow back and she is finally reunited with her husband and they live happily and in peace.

This story highlights the price that has to be paid for the devil's bargain. The success of the feminist movement of the twentieth century has finally allowed women to move into the male dominated world of work. Women can now compete as equals. Unfortunately the left-brain rationalist world is so strong that women have too often had to sacrifice the core of their femininity, the relational dimension. The masculine world, like the young king in the story, has fashioned silver hands for women. There is a deep psychology being expressed here. The hands represent a woman's ability to touch, to heal, to nurture. What a price to pay! The silver hands, though fashioned with good intentions, do not restore her to wholeness. They do not heal. They simply enhance her external appearance and make her functionally acceptable in the world of her husband.[36]

The Suppression of the Feminine

When applied to religious life it is easy to detect the silver hands that so many women religious have had to wear in the history of religious life. Women have long been encouraged to be passive and meek; to be subservient to the male dominated structures of the Catholic Church, and

---

[36] Barbara Fiand *Wrestling with God* p 63

frequently used as cheap labour. Often patronised as the *good sisters* they have not been allowed or encouraged to be true to their deepest selves. One of the saddest experiences in my religious life, is to hear good and dedicated male religious demean their female counterparts with disparaging remarks. I think this probably underlines the need men have to own all parts of themselves, and especially the feminine.

Whether men are from Mars or women from Venus we all inhabit the same universe! *Either/or* solutions are no longer adequate. Men too can see something of their woundedness in the myth of the handless maiden. As in the fisher king story the wound is revealed in the feeling function. Men also pay the price for the devil's bargain of living in a rationalist left-brain world and functioning efficiently. Many priests and religious today appear constantly tired and overworked. This may be due to the demands of ministry, but at a deeper level it expresses the inability to engage with *leisure* or with *play*. There is so much guilt stored here. This is all part of the devil's bargain.

The greatest price of all, however, is paid when the outer world so absorbs all our best energies that little is left for the inner journey. We can function well in that outer world but we do it with silver hands. Robert A Johnson makes this point well:

On closer examination this bargain is as painful to a man as to a woman, for it is often his inner tender qualities that pay the price. It is more difficult for a man to be aware of his inner nature because it is the young feminine – the most tender and sensitive parts of his inner nature – that is wounded. Virtually all of a man's feelings, sense of worth, sense of value, and moods are feminine. To wound the interior feminine in a man is to wound his whole feeling life and sense of worth. Since the feminine part of a man is usually less well developed than his masculinity, this sensitive part of his nature is often ignored and neglected. Most men are not even aware that it is their feminine side that is the keeper of all that is tender and precious in their lives! This means the naive, sensitive, largely unknown part of a man that bears the cost. It is the usual lot of a man paying the devil's price to feel unhappy, tense, or anxious without knowing what has

happened to him. This is the young feminine in its inarticulate woundedness, the miller's daughter. Whether the drama goes on within a woman or is played out in the interior feminine part of a man, the story is much the same.[37]

In answer to the question, 'Will we make it?' Johnson quotes Dr Jung's reply 'If enough individuals do their inner work.'

[37] *The Fisher King and the Handless Maiden* p 75-76

CHAPTER FIVE

The Wisdom of the Wound

One of the reasons why we prefer the outer journey is because the relentless round of action distracts us from the pain and the challenge of going within. The figure of Parsival in the Grail story was content to face external threats and dangers but he wasn't able to ask the deeper question about the meaning of it all. For religious life to recover its liminal and transforming energy in the post-modern world, there must be sufficient members who can face woundedness and brokeness with courage and above all trust in the process. Then the wounds of the hero become truly sacred. Without that transformation they become sources of festering anger and bitterness. Dealing with this pain and anger has become one of the key aspects of the postmodern crisis, which is very much a crisis of the isolated self. Many anguished people, who struggle with these issues, fill our tabloid newspapers with their cries and pleas for financial compensation for the wounds that life inevitably brings. In the media we see relentless and at times vicious attacks on the failings of public bodies and on individuals in the public eye. We have lost the ability to forgive and our anger is projected outwards.

In many ways the outer life was at its peak in the nineteenth century to be followed in the twentieth century by those prophetic figures, Freud and Jung, with their scientific attempts to study the unconscious. Great artists, novelists and dramatists, classic right-brain people, had long understood the need to confront both light and dark, to live with the tension of paradox and of mystery. Freud considered the shadow in its personal aspects whereas Jung also pointed to the collective shadow. With the work of these men and those who have built on their insights and refined and challenged them we are at last beginning to emerge from what Ken Wilbur calls the *flatlands of modernity.* For too long we have lived without a connecting story and the split between outer and inner has led to the dominance of *either/or* thinking. The links between matter, mind, soul and spirit were broken in favour of a much-reduced vision of reality in which science and technology ruled alone. Meanwhile the fisher king sought healing and the miller's daughter worked with silver hands:

The modern and postmodern world is still living in the grips of flatland, of surfaces, of exteriors, devoid of interior anything: "no within, no deep."[38]

A connected vision, which incorporates the left-brain awareness of paradox and mystery, is needed if we are to recover the great wisdom tradition that lies at the heart of all healthy religion. At its best this tradition provides an integrated pattern that excludes nothing. Everything is seen as part of the heroic journey, including and especially, the mistakes, the failure, the pain and the ugliness. We need to rediscover the wisdom in our woundedness.

The Spirituality of Perfection

While the modern world of the Enlightenment was rejecting soul and spirit, religion itself reacted in an unhealthy way by rejecting matter and even soul. Religious life in particular absorbed and passed on an incomplete spirituality, but one that became very widespread. Somehow it managed to override all the charisms of various Orders and Congregations and created a religious version of the flatlands. It might have been a spiritual flatland but it was still a flatland. It was largely negative and reactive: anti-world, anti-the human body, anti-sexuality, anti-friendship. This was particularly tragic and ironic for Catholic spirituality with its strong sacramental tradition. In effect we were promoting a spirituality that was almost denying the reality of the Incarnation. Jesus became fully human; we responded by wanting to become angels.

At the core of this flatland spirituality was the quest for perfection, and religious life itself was described as the *way of perfection*, or even the *state of perfection*. So whatever the disease, religious were the prime carriers! Unfortunately we seemed to have forgotten the wisdom of Theresa of Avila. Her classic Interior Castle describes the soul's many rooms; at the foundation of the mansion was self-knowledge. In fact she says that if you lack self-knowledge you are wasting your time trying to get into any of the other rooms! A healthy spirituality has to be rooted in what is true and real; it calls for honesty and awareness. It calls for awareness of the inner life. It calls for an awareness of what Freud and Jung called the shadow.

38 Ken Wilbur *The Marriage of Sense and Soul* (N Y Broadway Books 1999) p 139

We can see how a spirituality of perfection can take root. In the Gospel we find the words:

'You must therefore be perfect just as your heavenly Father is perfect'.[39]

Biblical scholars today explain how this word *perfect* in fact means complete. In other words it includes everything. But that was not the way it was generally interpreted. Much of our moral teaching in Christianity encourages us to improve, to be more generous, more hard-working, more just etc. Religious orders perhaps put more emphasis on this kind of *perfection* than anyone else. For example, in Jesuit documents, there is an exhortation to strive always for the magis (the more) and to do everything *ad majorem Dei gloriam* (for the greater glory of God). Sisters of St Joseph are given a hundred *maxims of perfection* to follow. Also held up for emulation have been young and idealistic saints, such as St Stanilaus Kostka whose motto was *ad majorem natus sum* (I was born for greater things).[40]

A great deal of hagiography further reinforced this message by portraying saints as being almost super-human and far removed from the everyday struggles of ordinary people. In many novitiates and houses of formation, religious in initial formation were encouraged and rewarded for seeking perfection. The Jungian analyst Marion Woodman suggests that this kind of perfectionism is another offshoot of our prevailing masculine consciousness. While non-believers seek satisfaction for their deepest hungers in various forms of addiction, believers can easily slip into a one-dimensional spirituality.

Essentially I am suggesting that many of us, men and women, are addicted in one way or another because our patriarchal culture emphasises specialisation and perfection. Driven to do our best at school, on the job, in our relationships - in every corner of our lives - we try to make ourselves into works of art. Working so hard to create our own perfection we forget that we are human beings.[41] According to Woodman the vital issue for the achievement centred perfectionist is how to restore the lost relationship to the heart.

---

[39] Matthew 5:48

[40] Wilkie Au and Noreen Cannon *Urgings of the Heart* (Mahwah N J Paulist Press 1995) pp 66, 67

[41] Marion Woodman quoted in Au and Cannon 1995 p 69

The Light and the Dark

One of the best ways to do this is to acknowledge that we are not perfect, nor are we meant to be. Our humanity is full of limitations and we need to embrace those limitations. We have to own the darkness as well as the light in our lives. It has to be *both/and* and not *either/or*. This is the message of that much-neglected passage in Matthew's Gospel, the parable of the wheat and the weeds.[42] When the servants asked the man in the story if they should root out the weeds that had grown with the wheat, the man replies with a clear 'No, let them both grow together.' Very few of us were taught that kind of soul-wisdom in our religious life formation programmes. One of the best ways to get in touch with the light and the dark within ourselves is to explore what Jung calls the shadow.[43]

The people who built our great cathedrals knew this kind of soul wisdom. Shortly after my visit to Ground Zero, which I described at the beginning of this book, I went to the great cathedral of St John the Divine in New York City. Cathedrals have a wonderful way of portraying the light and the dark of the spiritual journey. Alongside the soaring architecture that stretches the human spirit they often include strange carvings of gargoyles, grotesque figures that reflect darker aspects of our lives. In many of our cathedrals the misericords (small tip-up seats for the clergy to sit on) include all kinds of not particularly pious carvings such as a man and his wife quarrelling over a cooking pot, or a variety of animals. At the top of many vaulted ceilings you can find representations of comic figures, of a man being punished for stealing grapes, and of the village gossip silenced with a scold's bridle. As I wandered round the cathedral of St John the Divine in New York I was delighted to discover a side-altar dedicated to St Francis of Assisi. The statue itself was quite small; what really caught my eye was a large and fierce looking figure of a wolf.

The Story of the Wolf of Gubbio

In thirteenth century Italy there was a village on a hillside of great beauty whose people were duly proud of their idyllic home. Parents worked hard, children were well behaved. Some would call them arrogant because they rather despised their ill-kempt neighbours below them. Then one night a shadow came over the village and slaughtered two villagers. Two young

---

42 Matthew 13:24-30

43 For practical exercises in owning the shadow see John Monbourquette *How To Befriend Your Shadow* (Novalis Canada Darton Longman and Todd 2001) David Richo *Shadow Dance* (Boston Shambhala Publications 1999) Debbie Ford *The Secret of the Shadow* (London Hodder and Stoughton 2002)

men who volunteered to destroy the beast were likewise savagely killed. In real panic the village council decided to seek the help of a holy man who was rumoured to talk to animals. That man was Francis of Assisi. So a delegation was duly dispatched to implore his help.

On their way back to the village, Francis separated from them and entered the forest where the beast lived. Next day the villagers were impatiently waiting for him to emerge from the forest. Eventually he came slowly to the village fountain and addressed the crowd. "People of Gubbio, you must feed your wolf!" and then he left abruptly. The people were angry at this advice and very critical of this so-called holy man. They had wanted him to send the wolf to Perugia! But fear got the better of them. That night they left some food out in the street and continued to do so. No further attacks were recorded in the village of Gubbio. At the same time the villagers began to change, becoming less arrogant and more humble, as they acknowledged that the wolf was theirs.

Owning the Shadow

The work of Carl Jung seems to offer the clearest account of the shadow side of our personality. He places the shadow in the context of human development and it is this area of human growth and self-knowledge, which has become so significant in our understanding of ourselves in life's journey. All of us are ideally born into a world of unconditional love and acceptance especially from our mother. But as we grow we discover our parents and significant others seeming to place conditions on that love. We receive many messages telling us what not to do, how not to behave in public, what not to think, and even what not too feel etc. Wise parents and teachers will distinguish between a natural emotion such as anger, and its expression through violent behaviour. We need this socialisation, but we achieve it by hiding the qualities which don't seem to get rewarded.

Later these prohibitions, which are all a necessary part of the socialisation process, get further reinforcement from our teachers, and in religious life from those responsible for initial formation. What happens then is that in order to have our basic needs met, and to gain approval from significant others, we repress and hide all those parts of ourselves that are not acceptable. Religious life understood as the way of perfection strongly reinforced the image of the ideal religious: quiet, docile, very obedient, constantly working. Assertiveness or creativity had to be suppressed and any sexual thoughts or feelings were likewise viewed with alarm. Even friendship, one of the greatest human gifts, was discouraged. As we block off the unacceptable parts of ourselves we continue to develop our public persona. This is the ideal image of ourselves, seeking approval and recognition. The persona is strongly ego-controlled and above all it wants to be liked and to be successful. If early upbringing is full of frustrations a strong persona can block and damage emotional well being.

A Spirituality of Imperfection

The building of the persona is an essential task in the first half of life; it is all part of the outer journey. In the second half of life the challenge is to move inwards to connect with all parts of our personalities, especially the hidden ones. Unless this happens we cannot achieve wholeness. There are no perfect human beings, no perfect communities, no perfect marriages; we are both light and dark, wheat and weed, saint and sinner:

Inner work - the process of knowing, healing and harmonising our inner life - is the essence of spirituality because it is our inner life that influences our perceptions, desires, thoughts and actions. Ignoring the inner work because we do not like what we find, or postponing inner work out of fear of what we might discover, makes the shadow increasingly difficult to deal with.[44]

The shadow is not evil. It is only when the shadow is denied that it exerts a dark influence. Some say the greater the light the greater the shadow; hence the particular need for religious believers to own their shadow. If the shadow is denied then it will not disappear; what happens is that we project our darker side on to someone else. This happens so often in politics when one side projects all its evil onto another: we see this in different parts of the world, between Catholics and Protestants, between Palestinians and Israelis, and now between fundamentalist Moslems and the Christian West. The threat of terrorism and its fears have become daily realities. In the face of these global threats it is difficult to see what an individual can do. We often start life idealistically thinking we can change the world; what we are asked to do is to transform ourselves.

[44] Au and Cannon 1995 p 26, 27

It is all too easy to see how nations and other groups project their dark side onto others; individuals also play this game of scapegoating. Projection can just as easily take place within the setting of marriage or a religious community. Our postmodern world favours transient relationships, and is deeply scared of commitment. Structures, such as marriage or religious life, where we are bound by vow, help to provide the kind of boundary that allow our projection to be observed, to be owned and to be forgiven. If we can own our dark and light side then we are open to the forgiveness that only God can give. This is the good news operating in our lives, when we can place our brokeness and our woundedness into the heart and side of the wounded Christ.

From Projection to Acceptance

Once this starts to happen then in a very real sense we are free because we have nothing left to defend. Our failure has led to our biggest success because we are known and held as loved-sinners in the heart of God's forgiveness. This surely is the true purpose of religion when good and bad, light and dark, are owned and acknowledged instead of being projected onto another. We discover the gold in the heart of our shadow.

Then we realise that this public face that we have been cultivating, our good reputation, our standing before others, count for nothing. It is in fact the false self. What we have been slowly building for the first part of our life, the Lord now wants to pull down. This is the pain of the Paschal Mystery working itself out as the story of grace emerging in our lives. What now emerges is the true self at the intersection of light and dark in the core of our being. This is healthy religion:

> **The religious faculty is the art of taking the opposites and binding them back together again, surmounting the split that has been causing so much suffering. It helps us to move from contradiction - that painful condition where things oppose each other - to the realm of paradox where we are able to entertain simultaneously two contradictory notions and give them equal dignity. Then, and only then, is the possibility of grace, the spiritual experience of contradictions brought into a coherent whole, giving us a unity greater than either one of them.**[45]

[45] Robert A Johnson *Owning Your Own Shadow* (Harper San Francisco 1993) pp 84, 85

So it becomes clear that Gospel living leads us not just in the ascent but in a real descent. This is the part we find most difficult to accept. We have to fail. The Gospels seem to divide people into those who recognised their failure, their sinfulness, and those who did not. The story of the Pharisee and the Publican is a classic example of someone who was not aware of his shadow, and a humble man who was.[46] The Jewish tradition of scapegoating is part of this same experience. Today we see much of this shadow experience projected by films, by novels and very much by tabloid newspapers that ritually pry into and dissect the lives of celebrities or public figures. As soon as one victim is offered up and slaughtered another one is sought and vast sums of money are paid for kiss-and-tell revelations.

If we can own our shadow we might be able to end the confrontational element of masculine consciousness that constantly seeks to divide humanity into rival groups or tribes. Men too often project their shadow onto women, women onto men, a similar projection can occur between white and black, Catholic and Protestant, Muslim and Hindu, Christian and Muslim. A *both/and* consciousness will look for mutuality rather than confrontation, will seek to deal with the anger and violence in myself rather than project anger and violence onto others.

Community Life as a Place for Compassion

In religious life much of this shadow projection will occur in community. Because of the shift to a more relational spirituality, community life has received a lot more attention in the recent renewal process. I think it is becoming necessary for that process to include the light and dark sides of both individual and community life. Chapters and mission statements all too often focus on the ideal with more and more worthy demands. These can simply increase peoples' sense of guilt, or lead to widespread indifference to the whole process of renewal by document. Perhaps religious could gather occasionally to reflect not just on the strengths of their charism but also on its shadow side. I have to say that I am not aware of any religious congregation that has formally done this. I hope I am wrong.

---

[46] Luke 18:9-14

In many ways the current woundedness of religious life can provide a new opportunity for an honest appraisal of relational difficulties. The hunger for, and fascination with relationships, is strong in our postmodern world. At the same time there are real difficulties in sustaining these commitments. So instead of promoting an impossible kind of perfectionism, religious could demonstrate how to live compassionately, and in a less judgmental way, by owning up to our vulnerabilities and brokeness. Some might think that we are lowering our standards. In fact the opposite is true. We are getting closer to the heart of the good news. In the final analysis we cannot make ourselves holy or perfect. All we are asked to do is to open ourselves to the unconditional and endlessly compassionate forgiveness of God. The search for perfection is a game for the ego; true holiness is a gift of grace. Robert A Johnson quotes from remarks made in a lecture by the Jungian analyst and Episcopal priest John Sanford:

You must understand God loves your shadow more than he loves your ego.... In a showdown God favours the shadow over the ego, for the shadow, with all its dangerousness, is closer to the centre and more genuine.[47]

The Catholic Church has long promoted the Sacrament of Reconciliation which provides us with an opportunity to name our demons. The emphasis may have wrongly suggested that all our faults were wiped away. Certainly God's forgiveness is complete and full, but the evil doesn't go away. This is the *thorn in the flesh* identified by St Paul, and quoted by Jung. We have to name our demons. We must go on struggling with them, in the trust and faith that the redemptive love of God embraces us in the light and darkness of our humanity. The medievals understood this. In Durham Cathedral there is a flawed pillar built into the structure which symbolises Christ, the rejected figure who becomes the cornerstone of the building.

Celebrities, Saints and Heroes

Our postmodern world is uncertain and suspicious about sanctity. Yet the fascination remains. Instead, in a media-obsessed age, we project most of our hopes and dreams onto celebrities. People in the public eye have their lives scrutinised to a degree unheard of in any other culture. Inevitably their failings are exposed, and the press is often merciless in excoriating the

---

[47] Quoted in Robert A Johnson *Owning Your Own Shadow* pp 44, 45

failings of public figures. This is the new secular inquisition which masks a deep unease with human weakness. Most of all it reflects our own fear of failure. With no over-arching story to give meaning or pattern to the light and dark of our lives, we project all our anger and frustration on to someone else. The heroic path is never just a private journey. Everything is connected in the enchanted world that God has created for us. The heroes or heroines do not make the journey for themselves, as another example of postmodern lifestyle choice. The journey is for the human community; the hero must return to share the wisdom of the wound.

CHAPTER SIX

Community: Ideal or Real?

As we move into the twenty first century religious life is being called to answer the deepest hungers of our age. From all sides we are being reminded of the centrality of relationships and yet culturally most of our energy is directed into the outer journey. Yet the hunger is there. Contemporary cinema provides plenty of evidence with the enormous box-office successes of films such as Lord of the Rings, Star Wars and the Harry Potter stories, even though the focus is on the male heroic journey. These films stress the challenge of struggling with evil and fighting for a noble cause. They use myth, symbols and the power of imagination. Joseph Campbell has reminded us of the importance of the myth of the hero, but the missing link in the story, as it has unfolded in western culture, is the need for the hero/heroine to share their story with the community, rather than ride off into the sunset seeking another adventure. How this sharing is to take place, while respecting the integrity of the individual journey, is one of the critical questions in the renewal of religious community. The issues of life style and the need for a new balance between outer and inner also impinges on community life. So too the implications of a more rounded and real spirituality which integrates the light and the dark, the wheat and the weeds.

A New Look at Community

In the renewal of religious life the question of community has once again come to the fore. I think this is clearly connected to the relational shifts that are taking place in our culture. If community is such a key part of religious life then we should have something to say to the culture in which we live. Many of the issues involved have received thorough coverage in recent literature on religious life.[48] Patricia Wittberg points to the overwhelming evidence from many social critics that the deepest hunger of our individualistic western culture is:

a desire for community and spiritual depth.[49]

The struggles of religious in the area of community life may have something to contribute to the cultural debate. But a Gospel model of community needs to be rooted in a realistic and fully human spirituality, otherwise the

---

48 Patricia Wittberg *Pathways to Re-Creating Religious Communities* (Mahwah N J Paulist Press 1996). Barbara Fiand *Where Two or Three Are Gathered*. (N Y Crossroad 1992). Judith Merkle *Committed By Choice* (Minnesota: The Liturgical Press 1992). *Vita Consecrata* (Rome Vatican Press 1996)

49 Patricia Wittberg *Pathways to Re-Creating Religious Communities* p 82

widespread opting out of community life, currently operating in many religious congregations, will continue. This is not a criticism of religious living alone; as St Augustine remarked about the Church, there are many *within* who may be *without* and many *without* who may be *within*.

How Jesus Lived

When we read the Gospels, perhaps we have concentrated so much on the teaching aspect of Jesus' ministry, what he did, that we have missed the example of how he lived. This is a particular temptation for the culture in which we are living with its stress on doing over being. The recent renewal process in religious life is responding to this issue with a new awareness of, and attention to, the importance of community.

Chapter nine of Luke's Gospel begins with Jesus sending the twelve out on their mission to proclaim the Kingdom of God and to heal diseases. A few verses later however, we find this interesting passage:

> **On their return the apostles gave him an account of all they had done. Then he took them with him and withdrew to a town called Bethsaida where they could be by themselves.**[50]

The apostles were clearly happy to share their stories and experiences with Jesus and with each other. Jesus then decides to take them away from the mission, to spend time among themselves. This pattern of mission, followed by withdrawal from the crowds, occurs in several other parts of the Gospels. Jesus clearly felt the need for rest and recuperation in reaction to the demands of the crowds. This is not something we have considered very much in religious life. The work and demands of the mission get plenty of emphasis; much less is given to the human needs of the workers. Recently, when reflecting on this passage in a retreat context, a very experienced priest told me that it was an eye-opener to him to see this pattern in the Gospels. When he took time off he simply felt guilty. He is not alone in that feeling!

Perhaps the most surprising, and rarely quoted passage, occurs at the end of chapter four of Luke's Gospel when Jesus has left Simon's house at daybreak to find a lonely place to pray. The crowds find him and beg him to stay. He refuses their request, as he explains that there are other things he has to do. It is comforting to know that Jesus did not respond to every request, and knew how to say 'No'. A clear rhythm, however, can be

---

[50] Luke 9:10 See also Luke 5:16; Matthew 14:22; 15:39; Mark 8:13; John 2:12; 4:1

discerned between the demands of mission and the need for time together, for experiences shared and for prayer. Jesus is modelling a very balanced spirituality which reaches out to people in need, but doesn't forget the needs of the disciples. Jesus comes across in the Gospels as someone who knows how to balance the needs of the outer and the inner journey, the without and the within.

An Imperfect Community

A second theme which emerges from the community that Jesus gathers around him, is the need for continuous conversion. Even though the apostles had, in the Lord himself, the best possible novice master or formation director, they frequently get it wrong. Peter is described as a man of little faith; he is strongly rebuked by Jesus when he tries to deflect him from the passage of suffering. His betrayal of Jesus is graphically told. The disciples are portrayed as arguing among themselves as to which of them is the greatest; Jesus places a child before them, as an example of the need for simplicity and trust. On another occasion he is described as being angry with the disciples for preventing children from getting close to him. The mother of the sons of Zebedee provokes an argument as she seeks to promote her sons in the pecking order. At times Jesus seems exasperated at the lack of perception and understanding shown by the disciples. I find all of this deeply encouraging.

In relating the story of Jesus and his disciples, the evangelists make no attempt to cover up any of these weaknesses. It would seem that Peter, the appointed leader, was particularly concerned to have his mistakes fully reported. There are no spin-doctors around in the early Church. How different from our contemporary culture, where politicians rarely admit to making errors and so many Church leaders in recent times have been involved in the scandalous cover up of clerical child abuse. This latter sad situation seems to be a product of the spirituality of perfection mentioned in the last chapter. If we cannot own our dark side then we project it onto some other group. Some Church leaders have even blamed the media for attempting to get at the truth, as if the Church is beyond criticism. I hold no brief for the media, but the attempt to cover up and hide child abuse seems to be a clear case of shadow denial.

Pre-Vatican II religious life was strictly organised, very institutional and hierarchical, with little or no recognition given to the needs of the individual.

The Congregation always came first; the individual religious second. As one elderly sister said to me once, in pre-conciliar religious life you almost had to get permission to sneeze. When Vatican II stressed the dignity of the person it tolled the death knell for that highly regimented style of community life, although some pockets of resistance remain. After Vatican II the conservative model of community gave way to a less restrictive style. The liberal model may have been a necessary phase to grow through, but it is being seen as increasingly inadequate for the world in which we are living. While the Church was rightly promoting the dignity of the person, the shadow side of this has been the growth of individualism. This is another area underlined by the Nygren-Ukeritis observation, that religious are not sufficiently aware of the culture in which they live and move and have their being. Both modernity and postmodernity have promoted a very aggressive individualism. The consequence has been the breakdown and loosening of social bonds and community:

> **All of this leads us to consider the most serious limitation of liberalism: its inability to respond to a very deep human need for a common meaning and vision. People cannot live by freedom and tolerance alone. There is no salvation by interaction alone.**[51]

This lack of a common vision indicates a crisis of spirituality and hence the need for liminal groups to try to struggle with some of the issues involved.

Individualism

This shadow side of individualism has not received sufficient recognition in the renewal process, certainly in the documents that emerge from congregational get-togethers. As we anticipated and celebrated the first day of the new millennium I recall a concert at Greenwich on the banks of the River Thames in London. As midnight 2000 approached the singer Mick Hucknell delivered a song that for him summed up the dying twentieth century. It was Frank Sinatra's 'My Way'. What an inspired choice as we said goodbye to the most individualistic of centuries. Unfortunately many religious might have to admit that the song described an attitude all too prevalent in the way we now live.

In recent years it is being recognised that a new balance needs to be found between the legitimate needs of the individual and the demands of community. I am suggesting that most of us are still locked into a predominantly functional way of relating. We need to find a middle way or

---

51 Mary Jo Leddy *Reweaving Religious Life* (Mystic Ct. Twenty-Third Publications 1991) p 38

a more mature adult way of relating. We must move beyond the dependency culture of the conservative model while avoiding the excessive independence of the liberal one. A truly relational spirituality has to address this problem and find ways in which we can create community-on-mission, one that can recreate the Gospel pattern of mission and time-apart for sharing, for prayer and reflection, for celebration together and for rest. This shift of emphasis cannot be imposed these days but a common commitment to pastoral planning owned by the whole community seems to offer the best way forward.

The Need for Planning

Community planning allows us to agree on a common vision and goals in a way that the liberal laissez-faire model found difficult. In these days, when the model of one style of mission is unlikely to dominate community life, it provides a means of integrating the different missions of community members while honouring the one charism. It helps to move everyone from I to We, to a genuinely common ownership of what we are about. It can help get the balance right between the demands of mission and the demands of community, between the outer and the inner.

Here, as elsewhere, the model has to be *both/and* and not *either/or*. Part of the problem with the liberal model was an excessive emphasis on the therapeutic needs of the individual. This pushes the balance too far into the inner world to the detriment of the mission without. What then happens is that the community strays into the *soft feminine* and engages in too much navel-gazing and self-examination. The soft feminine can be a warm and inviting place to be, but it bears little resemblance to the challenge of building the Kingdom of God in the world. Sensible pastoral planning needs to include time for evaluation to ensure that the balance is right.

When reading the renewal documents of Chapters and Assemblies, it seems that there is little of the realism of the Gospel accounts referred to earlier. Chapters tend to be very idealistic and, while not wishing to be against idealism, this may account for the lack of interest many of these documents evoke from genuine and sincere religious. The often unspoken spirituality seems to owe more to the perfectionism alluded to in the previous chapter. This is not just a problem for religious life; it is cultural. It can be seen in the current obsession with measurable targets in just about every form of public life. Whatever target a school or a hospital achieves, they are immediately exhorted to do better. As targets get higher and higher one wonders what is supposed to happen when you reach 100%.

Paradoxically one of the strengths of contemporary spirituality is its discovery of the importance of weakness and failure. We are re-learning the ancient wisdom of soul that can embrace woundedness and brokeness, and see it as essential to experiencing the wonderful salvation and redemption that God offers us in Jesus, the rejected cornerstone. This helps to connect the soaring spirit of our idealism with our essential humanity, in what we call the humus that grounds our experience. Instead of chasing off with Parsival on yet another adventure, we are not afraid to connect with our wounded inner life and see how our very woundedness gives us a privileged access to the God of Jesus, who invites us to a spirituality of compassion.

The Golden Shadow of Individualism

In discovering the shadow we uncover the hidden gold. Judith Merkle has suggested that we need to discover the golden shadow of individualism in our community life.[52] This is true also of our collective shadow, and I think we can uncover it precisely in the area of mission, which draws so much of our time and energy. Instead of working and living in isolation, individuals are recognised as human beings with genuine needs. I have referred to the rhythm of ministry and withdrawal, modelled by Jesus in the Gospels, and also to the pattern of continuous conversion. Jesus is constantly drawing his disciples aside to explain what he is about, and as we have seen, correcting and challenging them to a deeper faith and love.

Practically every religious founder urged his or her followers to have special concern for the poor and the weak. It is worth asking why this is so. In the Gospels many of the religious leaders, who followed the letter of the law and the external rituals of religion, found themselves opposing the mission of Jesus. They had no need for God, because their religious practices gave them what they considered to be control of God. It was the poor and the weak, the lepers, the women, the children, the sinners and prostitutes, all the excluded groups, who, in their very vulnerability and brokenness, found themselves being embraced and loved unconditionally by Jesus.

---

52 Judith Merkle *Committed By Choice* (Minnesota: The Liturgical Press 1992) p 117

The Need for Failure

The danger in working for the poor is that our ego-needs often take over by setting us up as religious (the strong) working generously on behalf of the poor (the weak). I can recall when I first went, as young idealistic Salesian priest, to work in a socially disadvantaged area of Merseyside in the 1970s. I felt confident and enthusiastic about my mission to the young. I liked football, I liked popular music, I thought I had a good sense of humour. I was dedicated. I was going to be another Don Bosco! During that period of 14 years I soon discovered how little I knew about the world and the real needs of those youngsters.

It took me some time to realise that the poverty I needed to address was within myself. My own woundedness and inadequacies were being revealed. I needed to own them and even thank God for them. This is a lesson I am still struggling with many years later. We have to go down a long way! The descent of the spiritual life can be terrifying. It seems, that in the Gospel vision, we need to move into sharing some space with the poor, and to remain in that place so that we can recognise our deep inner poverty. The religious vow of poverty is a controversial one these days. In my experience whenever religious, or any people, get together to discuss poverty the temperature usually rises in the room as we try to play the game 'I'm poorer than you are'. I don't think we will ever resolve the anger that often surfaces in such discussions, unless we get down to the fundamental poverty of spirit in which we can embrace our whole selves, good and bad, light and dark, and hold that up to the Lord for healing and acceptance.

Jesus is constantly widening the circle in terms of Gospel mission. It includes the disciples themselves, it extends to all the excluded groups. Finally he suggests that we welcome the stranger and even love our enemies. This must include the enemy within, the stranger within, the parts of myself that I do not want to own or acknowledge. So we should never let the outer journey of mission take us away from the inner journey of owning all our human limitations and weaknesses. We can't really convert ourselves in this respect; this is the work of grace and grace is always a gift. But we can hopefully place ourselves with the excluded ones, to learn some of the right questions.

This to me is also what religious community is about. There is no such thing as an ideal community. Such a community would be highly dangerous! There are only real communities with real people, all of whom are wounded and broken in a variety of ways. Community may not be at its best when it appears to be successful and attracting all kinds of vocations. Maybe we need this period of contraction and weakness in churches and religious communities of the western world, so that we can really discover what Gospel poverty is about.

From Judgement to Compassion

We used to be trained for mission by being given all kinds of knowledge and information. Most formation programmes addressed our heads. So off we went with our left-brain missionary mind-sets only to discover a postmodern world that was already rejecting the myth of progress, the idea of the infinite perfectibility of humanity.

We cannot live the Gospel life in isolation. Sooner or later we have to engage with others. We have to gather in community, as fully open to the world in which we live. The postmodern world may not be quite sure what it wants. It is clearer on what it doesn't want. It certainly doesn't need people whose heads are filled with left-brain answers, who divide humanity into religious winners and losers. It is more likely to be impressed by men and women who look on the world with compassion rather than in judgement; who live in a community that can carry each others' burdens as well as work efficiently, because it is made up of men and women who have learned to accept all the limitations of being human and rejoice in that reality.

Instead of simply working harder and harder to minister to others in religious life we have an opportunity to model a community of flawed adults who know how to forgive each other. We learn to be ministered to and in that sense discover a pearl of great price. All of us need to be accepted at the deepest level of our being. A balanced life of mission and community helps us to create some space where our true poverty emerges as our greatest wealth, where we receive a level of acceptance that allows us to trust and reveal the deepest core of our humanity, the gift of true intimacy:
I shall not call you servants anymore.....I call you friends.[53]

53 John 15:15

CHAPTER SEVEN

Celibacy, Intimacy and Friendship

An over-investment in the outer journey reinforces the notion that the harder and more conscientiously we work, the more we will gain approval, both in the eyes of God and in the eyes of others. A realistic understanding of community however, should provide a more balanced picture. Excessive concentration on mission can still be an ego-game, unless it leads us into the kind of failure and awareness of our human limitations described in the last chapter. Work for the poor and marginalised is the best place for this to happen. In our postmodern world we are surrounded by the *relationally* poor, and it is vital that we see ourselves also in that category. Religious community can then be seen, not just as a service station for busy religious, but as a privileged place, a sacred space, in which we can befriend all aspects of our lives, good and bad, light and dark, and find acceptance. As we learn to carry the burdens of others in mission, so too our own limitations are shared and forgiven in community. This is the model of community which we find in the New Testament: one chosen by Jesus, to share in his mission while remaining a community in constant need of conversion and forgiveness.

In recent years, the traditional vows of religious life have, to some extent, been marginalised by our desire to put so much energy into mission. If we can redress the balance of our lives and achieve a better harmony then the vows can be understood as essential resources for both the outer and the inner journey. Their relevance to the world becomes clearer as we see the importance of intimacy which is at the core of a relational way of life. Poverty expresses our intimacy with our inner self; celibacy empowers us for intimacy with others; and obedience moves us into intimacy with the world.

The Gospel Pattern

I have referred to the number of occasions when Jesus withdrew with the twelve to spend what I suppose we would today call *quality time* with them, or *chilling out* to use the language of the street. But his desire for companionship and support went further than this. On more than one occasion he is seen to have a smaller and more intimate group of friends:

> **He took with him Peter, James and John and went up the mountain to pray.**[54]

When he enters the garden of Gethsemane he asks his disciples to remain behind:

> **'Stay here while I pray'. Then he took Peter and James and John with him.**[55]

The reference to John as the beloved disciple is clearly demonstrated in the intimate atmosphere of the Last Supper. What is also striking about the life of Jesus is the extraordinary freedom he demonstrated in his relationships with women. This is quite revolutionary for a male prophetic figure in the Jewish religious culture of his time. Scripture scholars today, enlightened by the long awaited contribution of feminist scholars, are painting a much richer portrait of the radical newness of Jesus in this respect:

> **It is remarkable how much material there is in the Gospels that gives a rather startling vision of how Jesus related to women, and enables us to come closer to his attitude to woman as such.**[56]

The Gospels describe Jesus touching the mother-in-law of Simon Peter, taking hold of the hand of a twelve-year-old girl, and therefore of marriageable age in contemporary Judaism. Jesus refuses to take the patriarchal masculine line of condemnation of the woman taken in adultery. We see his friendship with Martha and Mary and the other named women such as Mary Magdalene, Joanna, Susanna and others who accompanied him. The anointing at Bethany presents a most tender scene and is described in all four Gospels: it includes the anointing of the head, hands and feet. Luke's account describes the woman as a *sinner* and goes on to describe her actions with great intimacy: she washes the feet of Jesus with her tears, wipes them with her hair and covers his feet with kisses. Needless to say, the male onlookers are suitably shocked. It is ironic that when Jesus says that this woman's actions 'will be talked about for generations to come', unfortunately what seems to have survived is the shocked reaction of the onlookers, and a negative Christian understanding of women and their place in the Kingdom.

---

54 Luke 9:28

55 Mark 14:32-33

56 F J Moloney *Woman: First among the Faithful* (London Darton Longman and Todd 1985) p 8

The figure of St Paul is often presented in rather misogynist terms. This appears to be a superficial reading. Paul states his firm belief that Christian life is such a radically new experience-in Christ, that it wipes away all traditional distinctions:

There are no more distinctions between Jew and Greek, slave and free, male and female, but all of you are one in Christ.[57]

Paul goes out of his way to underline the radical equality that Jesus demonstrated should characterise life in the Kingdom:

'Who are my mother and my brothers?' And looking around at those sitting in a circle about him, he said, 'Here are my mother and my brothers. Anyone who does the will of God, that person is my brother and sister and mother.'[58]

Fear of the Body

Unfortunately, when we come to consider the vow of consecrated celibacy in religious life, we have to admit that much of the radical newness of the vision of Jesus and his freedom with women seems to get lost in a culture of fear and excessive caution. No one would want to deny that the whole area of human sexuality has to be approached with care and responsibility. But the negatives seem to have very quickly overwhelmed the positives in this area, and much of the liberating vision of Jesus was lost along the way. We are still suffering from this today. The Church seems to have been unduly influenced by the kind of dualism referred to earlier, which owes more to Greek philosophy rather than the values of the kingdom. A negative Manichean view of the body seems to have prevailed. Early on in Christian spirituality, for some reason, the healthy balance between spirit, body and soul got lost. Spirit was judged to be clearly superior to body, and the soul got sidelined.

Spirituality never exists in a vacuum, as recent studies in inculturation have made clear. Much of the Church's teaching in the whole area of sexuality seems to have been infected by a negative perception of women in particular and the body in general. Whenever the word friendship appeared, in my days of initial formation, it was always surrounded with negatives. It is easy to see how this kind of mind-set fed into the spirituality of perfection. Chastity was seen as the angelic virtue; any offence against

---

57 Galatians 3:28
58 Mark 3:34-35

chastity was viewed as gravely sinful. As a novice, I recall the advice: Raro unum, numquam duo, semper tres. (Rarely one, never two, always three) As the summer holidays approached one priest gave this gem of advice to seminarians: 'Avoid all women, especially those of the opposite sex'

Healthy Models

It is easy to present a simplistic black and white picture here, because there were notable exceptions to the negative view of friendship between the sexes in Christian history, pointing to a more rounded view of human life and experience. I have already referred to the balanced spirituality reflected in the architecture of our great cathedrals.

It is also fascinating to see the wonderful friendships that developed between some of our great saints and mystics: Jerome and Paula, Bernard of Clairvaux and the Duchess of Lorraine, Teresa of Avila and John of the Cross, Vincent de Paul and Louise de Marillac, Francis of Assisi and Clare, Philip Neri and Catherine of Reici, Francis of Sales and Jane Frances de Chantal. In view of some of our contemporary attitudes it is also worth noting the affectionate relationship between Augustine of Hippo and his male friend. He was clearly distraught at his death:

With what sorrow my heart was darkened. Everything in view looked like death. My native place seemed like torture, my father's house sheer unhappiness. Whatever I had talked about with him, now that he was gone, seemed like awful torment. My eyes looked everywhere for him and could not find him.[59]

The saints and mystics achieve greatness because of their passionate love for God. But in Christian spirituality that love can never be separated from love of neighbour. Nor can it be flattened out into a kind of passionless, vague love of mankind. For these holy men and women their growth in their journey to God seems to have involved genuine warmth and love for particular people:

Francis de Sales knew that relationships do not simply support us they shape us as well.....Francis knew that in their reaching out in friendship he and Jane mirrored for one another their widest capacities as human beings and encouraged one another in the necessary expansion to realise those capacities.[60]

[59] Augustine Confessions Book IV in *The Confessions of St Augustine* translated by E M Blaiklock (London Hodder and Stoughton 1983) p 84

[60] Wendy M Wright *A Retreat with Francis de Sales Jane de Chantal & Aelred of Rievaulx* (USA St Anthony Messenger Press 1996) p 48 49

The love that these friends had for each other did not block their love for God; it sustained and nourished it because it was rooted firmly in the God who is the ground of all love.

Care and Caution

Care and caution are always necessary in this delicate area, but they should not be allowed to destroy the gift and joys of genuine friendship. In recent years the Catholic Church has been shocked and shamed by scandals of sexual abuse. This is a complex matter, which is still unfolding in our midst, and we have to admit that some of the warnings of the past cannot just be ignored. During the period when I was involved in province leadership I remember a lawyer commenting on the difference between our pre-Vatican II and our post-Vatican II Constitutions in the area of chastity. Our old Salesian constitutions contained some very practical advice from our founder Don Bosco. Our new constitutions, published in 1984, removed all this material in reflecting a more optimistic liberal interpretation. In view of the recent tragic events, the Church and religious orders have had to return to more explicit guidelines. As with everything it is always a question of balance.

Relational Wholeness

Having made those caveats I still think that there is a need to place consecrated celibacy in a positive framework. To return to the pattern of the two journeys, a balanced spirituality requires a genuine attempt to integrate the masculine and feminine dimensions of our sexuality. Both philosophy and theology today are emphasising the relational as being at the core of what makes us human. Even science, in the field of quantum physics, is revealing how everything that exists is in a mysterious and profound relationship. We have moved on from the mechanistic Newtonian world of billiard-ball atoms moved by external forces. Our theology promotes communion as reflecting the intimate life of the Trinity itself.

Sadly these insights have not really penetrated into how many of us live. This is because the primary myth that controls our culture is an economic one. That is why so much energy goes into the outer journey, the masculine world of competition, of ever-increasing demands to produce more, so we can satisfy our needs by consuming more. There is a real danger that religious too can get sucked into the world of consumer culture, as we seek the latest and the best of what can be purchased by our credit cards. The greater temptation, however, is that we get so taken up by the demands of the mission, we are unable to say 'no' to the many requests we receive. After all it is nice and affirming to be wanted. The Messiah complex is alive and well in religious life. What suffers, however, is our inner life. The price is an inability to establish true intimacy with our inner self. Without a true sense of our own identity it is difficult to establish true intimacy with others and with God.

One of the saddest Gospel incidents for me is the remark of the elder brother of the prodigal son who is unable to share in the joy of the forgiveness offered by their father:

> **Look, all these years I have slaved for you and never once disobeyed your orders.**[61]

What a sad way to describe his relationship with his father: slavery! Sometimes in religious life you meet hard-working men and women for whom this phrase may sum up their apostolic lives. They frequently find themselves without friends. I remember arranging a funeral for a very dedicated religious; when I looked at his list of people he would like to be informed in the event of his death I found one name.

The Need for Intimacy

The need for intimacy has received much emphasis in recent psychological and spiritual literature. Developmental psychology has stressed the need for integration of all aspects of our humanity, the physical, the emotional, the intellectual and the spiritual. Pope John Paul's post–synod document on Religious Life states that consecrated life today has to be:

> **lived by men and women who show balance, self-mastery, an enterprising spirit, and psychological and affective maturity.**[62]

Reflecting on this quotation I was struck by the phrase *enterprising spirit* because it wasn't always associated with the way the vows were presented, and it seems to fit the heroic journey which I have been highlighting in this book.

[61] Luke 15:29

[62] *Vita Consecrata* n 88

Religious who can embark on this journey to intimacy may have something prophetic to say to a culture that is almost sated by a trivialised promotion of sex-as-fun. In the great stories and myths of the past the hero had to go out and risk the journey of adventure. After the inevitable wounding and failures, and false trails, he is led back home with a new and more integrated vision, one that includes all aspects of his human life and development. Often towards the end of this adventure he has to meet and befriend the feminine, what Jung called the anima. Too often in our Hollywood films, that create our modern and postmodern myths, the man and woman engage sexually almost from the start. The whole adventure of masculine and feminine relating, with its journey of discovery in a maturing relationship with all its joys and frustrations, gets foreshortened to the detriment of both masculine and feminine growth.

All of us are invited to make this journey into the inner world. It is a world which recognises our deep human need for affection, for affirmation, for joy, for space to grieve, for play and for laughter, for real communication from the core of our being. It is possible for same sex friendships to meet many of these human needs and experiences. One would hope that in the kind of open, honest and trusting communities, talked about in the last chapter, this will happen. But for this journey to touch the deepest depths in our humanity, our sexual identity, it seems not just advisable, but important, to develop healthy heterosexual relationships.

Friendship as Prophetic

Clearly these relationships cannot go down the path of genital intimacy. I remember a talk given by Cardinal Basil Hume at the Conference of Religious for provincials in Britain when he spoke of the need to recover words like friendship and intimacy and take them out of the narrow constraints of our very sexually charged culture, which equates intimacy with genital experience. Part of this recovery would be to recognise that all of us need the human touch:

> **Everyone needs loving touches. Touch is our most basic and earliest form of communication. It is the method of communication necessary in infancy to convince us that we are loved, needed and accepted. This need remains throughout our lives.**[63]

---

63 Donna Tiernan Mahoney *Touching the Face of God* (Dublin The Mercier Press 1991) p 76

Naturally, in these fraught days of heightened concern about inappropriate sexual behaviour, we need to show sensitivity and responsibility. The old cautions of previous formation would translate today into respect for people's legitimate boundaries. Nevertheless we have to be clear that consecrated celibacy is not served by religious robots, who remain closed to any expression of human warmth and feeling.

Some might argue that religious who develop heterosexual friendships are just seeking a good time, a bit of fun and relaxation from the grind of work and apostolate. In many ways this is often the model put forward in the postmodern culture which promotes playing the field, while avoiding any serious commitment. I think this would be a serious misunderstanding of the personal investment which is needed, if such relationships are to get beyond the trivial. A genuine relationship often involves real pain as two imperfect people struggle to deal with issues of growth and trust. That is why some level of self-intimacy is needed in any relationship.

Friendship for Growth

The male/female attraction initially triggers what is called the positive shadow when another person seems to carry a kind of magical attraction. This time of enhanced awareness and aliveness is not to be dismissed as mere infatuation. The sense of affirmation and worth it brings allows the individual to uncover unrealised gifts. The magical qualities that we see in another give life to the magical qualities I didn't suspect I had. With this new awareness of my inner goodness and beauty I am empowered to face the darker aspects of the self. Persevered with, this relationship will provide opportunities for the negative shadow to emerge. This is the time of real growth. As in the great mythical journey of the hero/heroine there is no adventure without setbacks, without pain, without wounds. It is the time for genuine integration and for acceptance of all aspects of who we are.

It might be argued that traditional community life should provide for all our intimacy needs. I am not convinced that we can make this claim. The traditional pattern of single sex communities does not seem to be able to provide this level of growth and intimacy. As we have seen from the Gospels, Jesus had friendships outside the community of the disciples, and even the twelve. What, however, is important for religious, is to have some form of accountability for their relationships, whether it be a spiritual director, or a trusted person. Accountability is one of the best ways to find the necessary balance between the lack of personal freedom in pre-conciliar religious life, the conservative model, with the excessive individualism of the liberal model. It also needs underlining that a friendship with someone outside the community must never interfere with a person's primary commitment. Relationships which call that into question are moving into dangerous territory. The whole point of consecrated celibacy is not that we do not love anyone, but that we do not love possessively.

As I approach almost forty years in religious life I can look back at the variety of Salesian communities I have lived in. I have had my periods of difficulty and honestly found one or two of my companions difficult to live with, as I am sure they have me. But my overwhelming memory is of much joy and laughter and genuine brotherhood. In every community I have discovered real friends. Outside of community, I have also been blessed by close women friends who have taught me so much about receiving and giving love. From them also, alongside my brothers, I have learned, and am still learning, what it means to be a priest, a religious and a man in this rapidly changing, puzzling, yet enchanted world in which we live.

To Know is to Love

To return to the Gospels, we find Jesus asking two very direct questions in the area of what we today call relational spirituality. The first question is:

Who do you say I am? [64]

And the second which is repeated three times for emphasis:

Do you love me? [65]

These questions deal with the issues of identity and intimacy which close relationships put before us. They are both risky questions because they open us to the possibility of rejection. What I find interesting about the second question, famously asked of Peter, is that Jesus wants to make it crystal clear, in preparing Peter for leadership, that all ministry is rooted in a relationship of knowledge and love. He also seems to be saying, to our world of technological rationalism and objectivity, that true knowledge can

[64] Mark 8:29

[65] John 21:17

never be separated from what is deeply personal. Jesus knew what it was to operate out of both right and left brain. He had put it all together, yet this ability to open himself in vulnerability to others, meant that he was prepared to accept the joys and sorrows of intimate relationship.

His first question, 'Who do you say that I am?' led him immediately into the first prophecy of his Passion. The second question is recorded in John's Gospel immediately after the Risen Lord, in a scene of great familiarity, prepared breakfast for his disciples on the shore of Lake Tiberias. In an interesting echo of the earlier question the Gospels point out that:

> **None of the disciples was bold enough to ask, 'Who are you?';**
> **they knew quite well it was the Lord.**[66]

What seems to be happening here, is the revelation that God himself so enters into all aspects of human love, and in doing so, shows that authentic human love must be open to vulnerability, and the breaking of the human heart. Peter reacted badly to Jesus' first prophecy of Passion and Death. Not surprisingly he failed to understand. In the Resurrection Appearance the disciples now know the Lord at a new level. Peter himself is asked to respond to the Lord's invitation to love in a new way. They have all experienced failure, they abandoned the Lord in their different ways. Now as wounded men they are being loved, forgiven and commissioned to carry this message to the world.

Jesus now has at his service a community of wounded men, who have experienced something of their own poverty of spirit in their inability to be faithful to their Lord and Master in the time of crisis. Yet their experience of his acceptance and forgiveness, and a renewed offer of friendship has led them to an even deeper level of knowledge of who he was. One of the joys of friendship and community is the joy of a shared meal. What a wonderful picture of intimacy is presented to us at that breakfast by the shores of the lake.

Celibacy and Poverty

The purpose of consecrated celibacy is to highlight the essential journey of discovery into the human heart. We do not serve the celibate vocation by remaining aloof from human warmth and affection. A journey to the heart brings its joys and sorrows, and both are necessary if we are to live the spirituality of compassion modelled by Jesus. I have suggested that religious life, as a liminal calling, has to address the hungers of our time. The relational hunger of our culture is laid bare for all of us to see. We share it too. Since no merely human relationship can fully satisfy the deepest hunger of the human heart, limitation and incompleteness is built into all our human experiences. Happiness is always transitory. Even peak experiences cannot last forever. Life, in its humdrum reality, has to go on. In the story of the miller's daughter, even the love of her husband, the king, could not bring healing to her silver hands. For that to happen, she had to enter the forest and stay in solitude. In religious life the forest experience is provided by the vow of poverty, which is like the other side of the coin of chastity. It is only when we are truly emptied and hollowed out, in other words, truly poor in spirit, that we can be ready for what we are made for: the direct experience of God's unconditional love. This is not something we can bring about by our activity, however good, it is a gift of grace.

CHAPTER EIGHT

Poverty, Contemplation, and Intimacy with God

The outer and inner journeys can only be fully understood as two aspects of the same journey. The Christian pilgrimage is truly described as the quest for God. This is the basic human quest in every age. It is a journey from the head to the heart. I have suggested that this is the whole purpose of consecrated celibacy. The Church and the world need some people, who by taking specific vows, express liminal human values, and thereby become icons for the rest of humanity. Religious cannot claim to live a *state of perfection*. We are all wounded people, and we need to own that brokeness, rather than project it onto others. The vows are a public sign of the commitment to the universal human journey towards that intimacy with God, for which we have all been created, and which begins and ends in the human heart.

A reflection on the vows can only really be placed in the context of all three vows. In a sense we are looking at three sides of a triangle: take one away and the whole thing collapses. In this chapter I want to look at the vow of poverty, but only in the context of what was said in the last chapter about consecrated celibacy. This leads naturally into a reflection on obedience in chapter nine. I don't think it is possible to live a holistic celibacy, without confronting the issue of poverty. In the postmodern consumerist culture in which we live, such vows have more not less relevance.

The Vows as Inner Experiences

I have referred to the phenomenon of good and observant religious often getting angry when debating aspects of poverty, particularly what I would call the outer journey of the mission to the poor and the poverty of life-style expected of vowed religious. Why is this so? I think it may have something to do with a dualistic interpretation of the vow. If we simply see it in external, measurable terms, we drift very easily into an all too masculine understanding. Our extraverted masculine culture favours domination, the will to power and clear lines of superiority. There can be no doubting Luke's version of the first of the beatitudes:

How happy are you who are poor; yours is the kingdom of God.[67]

A certain simplicity of life-style and a commitment to work for those in need, is central to apostolic religious life. But the ego is so strong that, if we are not careful, we can allow our poverty and our work for the poor to make us feel superior to others. That is why we have to include Matthew's version of the beatitude which says:

How happy are the poor in spirit; theirs is the kingdom of heaven.[68]

It is Matthew's version which I think leads us to face up to the personal poverty at the core of our being. Matthew and Luke together help us to a *both/and* interpretation. In some ways the in-depth acceptance of our own poverty can be more difficult to acknowledge than pouring ourselves into service of others, if that service reinforces the sense that we religious (the strong) are working for those in need (the weak). What we have to own, at the deepest level of our being, is what has been called our ontological poverty

The Attack on Jesus' Humanity

In this respect one of the key passages in the Gospels is the account in the synoptics of the three temptations of Jesus. What is fascinating about Satan's assault on Jesus is that he attacks Him in His humanity. The temptations are aimed at exposing the limitations and inherent weakness of human existence. Jesus rejects the temptation to achieve success by magic, by seeking the spectacular, or by claiming earthly power and possessions. What Satan is afraid of is the powerlessness of God manifested in the loving and compassionate heart of Jesus:

Satan fears the Trojan horse of an open human heart that will remain true to its native poverty, suffer the misery and abandonment that is humanity's and thus save humankind......
He came to us where we really are – with all our broken dreams and hopes with the meaning of existence slipping through our fingers. He came and stood with us, struggling with his whole heart to say "yes" to our innate poverty.[69]

---

[67] Luke 6:20

[68] Matthew 5:3

[69] Johannes Baptist Metz *Poverty of Spirit* (Mahwah N J Paulist Press 1998) pp 11, 14

The great story of Genesis reveals the fear and insecurity of the human heart, as Adam and Eve accept the serpent's invitation to taste the fruit and become like gods, knowing good from evil. We want to be human in a god-like way.

The Hollowing Out of the Ego

In a sense the whole of our life's journey is an attempt to return to Eden. But we resist it and seek security and happiness, not just in material goods, in the promotion of the false self, and perhaps more subtly through religion and even good works. The Pharisees clung to the security of the Law, as they resisted Jesus' invitation to live a spirituality of the heart. Perhaps the culture of the masculine outer journey has placed too much of our spiritual journey in the area of external works. This might be fine for the first part of our lives, but as we enter the second part of life's journey we need to reconnect with the depth dimension of the mystery at the heart of human existence; we need to go within. We need to face our essential poverty. The word person comes from two Latin words *per* and *sonare* which means to sound through. Our lives have to include a hollowing out of the ego, as we learn to own our deep inner poverty.

A Sense of Shame

In chapter seven we discussed how we grow in knowledge of ourselves in and through relationships with others and how this degree of intimacy is not truly possible without a degree of self-intimacy. The beauty of friendship is revealed in the fact that we are loved and accepted because of who we are, not because of what we do.

In my experience of working with religious in the context of retreats, it seems to me that this level of acceptance is difficult to achieve. Human love can take us so far, but as St Augustine reminds us, our hearts are made for God and will not rest until we find that love in the heart of God. Reflecting on my own experience, and that of others, I think that many of us feel a sense of shame when we think about our inner selves. This sense of inadequacy and shame is rooted in personal sinfulness and reinforced by a lifetime of the negative judgements we may have experienced. The only place where this can be healed is in prayer. The importance of touch, which I addressed in the last chapter, now assumes a deeper dimension.

So many of the miracle stories of Jesus involve touch. It is as if Jesus knows our woundedness at a very deep level, and he is aware that his teaching cannot truly change lives unless we are healed and accepted at this profound level of human poverty and limitation. If our hearts truly are made for God, then only the healing love of God can penetrate our deepest poverty and woundedness. All of us experience this deep poverty in our own way. There are aspects of our shame that we do not want to share with others.

A few months ago I found myself walking through Harlem in New York City. I was on a pilgrimage; my destination was the Church of Corpus Christi on West 121st Street. I wanted to visit this Church because it was there in the autumn of 1938 that Thomas Merton was baptised and received into the Catholic Church. Like so many others, I have long admired and been fascinated by the life of Merton, who in the twentieth century really modelled the heroic journey, and as a gifted writer, he has shared his story with the world. It was a hot humid summer day in New York and as I reached the church I found it locked. With the kindness of one of the parish secretaries, I eventually found myself alone in the church in prayer just a few feet away from the baptistry where Merton was baptised, and the confessional where he made his first confession. After some time I began to weep almost uncontrollably. My whole body began to shake. I became acutely aware of a level of acceptance and love which embraced every aspect of my own sinfulness and limitations. I felt I was being embraced and touched by God in a way that went beyond human touch. It is difficult to put words on such an experience. I think I now know what the phrase *gut reaction* means. I have had similar experiences in other sacred spaces. Healing can never be a one-off event; we stand in the need of continuous conversion. Our sin never goes away; what weakens is its power to oppress us.

Prayer as the Place for Acceptance and Healing

The primary place for this to happen in our spiritual journey is prayer. As we obey Vatican II's call to read the signs of the times in this seemingly secular postmodern age, one of the most striking and dramatic developments in recent years has been the re-discovery of contemplative prayer. As we are leaving the flatlands of modernity it seems that the long hidden hunger for contemplative prayer is re-emerging in the world. For many centuries contemplative prayer was part of the ordinary experience of all Christians. The cultural changes of the Protestant reformation, the rise of science and the rationalism of the Enlightenment, all conspired to blot it out of ordinary consciousness. Right-brain thinking took control with its categories of analysis, of manipulation, its drive for what it considered to be objectivity.

Even in the church we responded by neglecting this great journey into the wisdom of the heart in favour of rationality alone. The Church put most of its energy into educating the laity and the young, into rational answers and the search for Catholic certainties. We had the truth and all we had to do was to defend it; we had no place for the spacious territory of the heart where paradox and symbol live. We were in a battle and we had to win it in a typically masculine, confrontational style. Parsifal didn't need to connect with the fisher king; he had too many battles to fight defending Catholic truth. In the meantime the feminine was operating with silver hands.

The Third Millennium is for Mystics

In the seventeenth century my Salesian patron, Francis of Sales, made a great effort to open up the ways of holiness to the ordinary laity, an issue which has come to the fore again since Vatican II. In the twentieth century it was Thomas Merton, who perhaps more than anyone, opened up the invitation to contemplative prayer to everyone. We need to see this movement as going to the essence of the spiritual journey. It can heal the too-rigid division between active and contemplative religious life. Despite opting for a life of seclusion in a Trappist monastery in the rolling hills of Kentucky, Thomas Merton became one of the most prophetic voices of the twentieth century, as he addressed the contemporary issues of racism, nuclear war and the need for inter-faith dialogue. He gave fresh voice to the ancient tradition of Christian non-violence. With the current threats from fundamentalism, the need for non-violent living and understanding is more necessary than ever.

It is no surprise that the dualism that has dominated our recent culture took hold precisely when the unifying gift of contemplative wordless prayer fell into neglect. I am certainly not suggesting that prayer was extinguished in the Church. But contemplative prayer which has traditionally been viewed as the highest form of prayer was left largely to the enclosed orders and congregations.

What our fragmented world needs today is a return to the Sacred Feminine, to that place of wisdom which we discover in the core of our being, in our vulnerable and wounded hearts. That means our hearts can provide space for the humble recognition of our need for God. This is the purity of heart that Jesus speaks of in the beatitudes:

> **The third millennium: a time for mystics! It will be the depth of men and women moved by the Spirit that will save the meaning of life and challenge the limitations of our human vision.**[70]

A capitalist, over masculine spirituality, can give the false impression that with our good deeds and actions we can gain God's favour. We cannot gain what we already have. Jesus tells us in the Gospels that eternal life is now. It is a gift to the meek and poor in spirit. The purpose of the human journey is to reach the point where we become aware that we are loved unconditionally by God. God's love is pure gift; it is not something we can earn. We Catholics have a word for it: it is grace. What we are asked to do is to put on a contemplative mind that sees everything as gift and a source of thankfulness. This is eucharistic living.

A Gift for All

We don't have to be special to be contemplatives:

> **Contemplation provides the loftiest moments in prayer. But, as Vita Consecrata tells us, it is not the privilege of a certain state, but an essential dimension in those who feel their life 'transfigured' in Christ.**[71]

All we have to do is accept the limitations of who we are in God. We do not have to live a kind of double life: ordinary life with its eating and sleeping, its work and play, the rhythm of the days and weeks and seasons, and then a kind of rarefied world of religious activities such as going to church and carrying out practices of piety. All is one; life is life. To be spiritual simply means being aware of how God is present in all human experiences, the

[70] Juan E Vecchi *Acts of the General Council of the Salesian Society of St John Bosco* (Rome Editrice SDB Jan-March 2001 N 374) p 19

[71] Juan E Vecchi p 16

joyous and beautiful ones, and the darker more painful ones. This is the Great Mystery which is bigger than any of us; it is what the Church calls the Paschal Mystery. It is the only pattern that Jesus left us.

Prayer, therefore, is not just another *holy* thing to do. It is simply a way of living in the presence. God is always present to us; if He were to stop thinking about us we would cease to exist. True spirituality is always about seeing. All we have to do is to get our egos out of the way and live in the spirit of the beatitudes:

> **What if we were to let go of the idea of prayer as a desire to establish contact with the deity in order to ask for forgiveness, for healing, for protection? What if we were to see it, rather, as the recognition and the desire to further what is; as a dwelling in, rather than an approaching? What if prayer were a continuous thanking for the reality that embraces us – a seeing and a celebrating of the Light by which we are surrounded? What if prayer flowed in us very much as our blood does – as a constant "yes" to life and to love, a perpetual affirmation and surrender – not anything we do but rather everything we are?**[72]

Such an approach to prayer moves us away from an understanding of prayer as talking to God which has long been, and still is, the predominant Catholic understanding of prayer. Catholics and religious still accuse themselves in confession of distractions in prayer. The problem with this is that it equates prayer with thinking, with what is going on in our heads. We are back in the left-brain stranglehold.

We apostolic religious owe a great deal of gratitude to the monastic tradition of religious life because since the Reformation and the Scientific Revolution they have kept alive the true nature of prayer. In a sense they, and many others, were living in the depths of the forest where the miller's daughter needed to find healing. In the immediate aftermath of Vatican II many religious orders made such a strong commitment to social activism on the part of the poor that they found themselves facing burnout and exhaustion. In response to this in the 1970s the major religious superiors in the USA turned to the monasteries, to men like Thomas Keating and Basil Pennington, Cistercians who themselves had been inspired by the figure of

---

[72] Barbara Fiand *Prayer as the Quest for Healing*
(N Y Crossroad Publishing Company 1999) p 5

Thomas Merton. They passed on Merton's method of Centring Prayer which is a form of prayer without words, which invites the individual to drop all personal agendas and simply to be in the presence of the Lord. The gift of wordless prayer and of contemplation is now much better appreciated in the Church and not just as the special vocation of a spiritual elite, but as a gift to all.

Prayer Without Words

The Church has always promoted many forms and styles of prayer: liturgical prayer, meditation, the divine office, the rosary etc. All these forms use words, images and symbols as we seek to communicate with God. In more contemplative prayer we move beyond words to simply being in the presence of God. Strictly speaking, contemplation is not something we can make happen; it is a gift of God. It is clear from the Gospels that the disciples were struck by the number of times Jesus withdrew from his active ministry to simply spend time in the presence of his Father:

Large crowds would gather to hear him and have their sickness cured, but he would always go off to some place where he could be alone and pray.[73]

The word always is an interesting one; some translations use often. What is clear is that this was very much the pattern:

Now it was about this time he went into the hills to pray; and he spent the whole night in prayer to God.[74]

Maybe what Jesus is trying to teach us is that all mission is rooted in relationship with the Father. What else is the kingdom about? We can get so caught up in the demands of mission and they are always so real and pressing, that we forget what it is all about. We get so taken up with working for God, working for others, talking about God, even reading about God, or theologising about God that we neglect what Jesus himself called the one thing necessary: a direct experience of God's presence.

Contemplation does not take us away from life in the world. It truly centres us so that we can live it to the full:

It is life itself, fully awake, fully active, and fully aware that it is alive. It is spiritual wonder. It is spontaneous awe at the sacredness of life, of being.[75]

[73] Luke 5:16
[74] Luke 6:12
[75] Thomas Merton *Selected Writings* edited by Christine M Bochen (N Y Orbis Books Maryknoll 2000) p 58

Poverty as the Way into Prayer

The vow of religious poverty remains at the heart of religious life. Not just because of the need to live simply in a world of great divisions between the materially rich and poor, but also because it asks us to confront the poverty of our very humanity in the face of a transcendent God. When we bring that poverty before the Lord, especially in moments of prayer, we meet the unconditional mercy and forgiveness of God. This journey requires a self-knowledge that demands real courage and an acknowledgement of our broken hearts. We then meet God as our saviour. Merton expresses this eloquently:

> **Mercy is the thing, the deepest thing that has been revealed to us by God. A mercy that cannot fail. It is precisely here that we come to a centre of Christian experience, a centre from which we can understand everything else.....**
>
> **What leads you into this centre is a life of prayer. At this centre you will experience the love and mercy of God for yourself and find your true identity as a person to whom God has been merciful and continues to be merciful.**
>
> **What leads up to this discovery is self-knowledge. I must find myself, I must solve my identity crisis, if I have one, then find myself as one loved by God, as chosen by God, and visited and overshadowed by God's mercy.**[76]

The journey into poverty, into the forest of private prayer and reflection, leads me into a space where I can experience the consolation of God's love and mercy. I can then live a life of love for others, with the power to give and receive friendship in a life of consecrated celibacy. We undertake the inner journey of discovery to know God's love as the ground of all reality. From there we can move out into creating God's kingdom in the world.

It is the vow of obedience which prevents our love from becoming too insular, too in-house. This is always a temptation for religious life. In contrast the genuine journey within, gives us the strength, energy, compassion and love to engage afresh in the journey without. It is obedience which summons us to intimacy with the world that God has created.

[76] Thomas Merton *Selected Writings* p 88

CHAPTER NINE

Obedience as Intimacy with the World

The three vows of religious life can only be properly understood together. I have stressed their relational character. Consecrated celibacy is an invitation to intimacy with others, but if it is lived honestly and courageously it leads us into an intimacy with ourselves, which is a depth experience of poverty of spirit. Life itself is the teacher here, as we come to terms with our inevitable failures and woundedness. Rather than deny this harsh reality, if we take it into the spaciousness of humble and contrite prayer, we learn a level of acceptance and forgiveness which helps to reduce the controlling power of our ego and moves us into the depths of the true self. This is the goal of the spiritual journey; it takes us into an experience of the Grail, the healing power of the Paschal Mystery of Jesus. Our wounds become sacred wounds instead of sources of anger and bitterness at life's unfairness.

From Within to Without

Such is the journey within, but I have stressed throughout how we cannot remain here. When we meet the Lord in the contemplative centre of our heart, we are filled with compassion and fired with the love of Christ, we are led back into the demands of ministry, to the journey without, into the world. One of the great misunderstandings of the masculine left-brain mentality, taken alone, is that we think that time spent in prayer is time taken from precious ministry. I think many religious feel this as a dilemma: either prayer or work. This stems from *either/or* dualistic thinking. The journey to the centre cannot take us away from our brothers and sisters in need. In fact it can only take us closer. This is the journey that Thomas Merton demonstrates in the clear shift from his early writings where he dismissed the world as of little interest and account, to the prophetic and fully engaged writings of his later life.

The vow that takes us into the world of mission is the vow of obedience. I think that this vow has changed more radically than any other in the renewal years since Vatican II. Many older religious will recall how this vow took away any kind of responsibility and creativity. There was little opportunity or encouragement to think critically or to pursue any personal agenda. The traditional style of obedience was immediate and unquestioning; of course it created a culture of dependency and immaturity. These criticisms have been well documented in much post-conciliar writing on religious life. What is more to the point is the way, as with other aspects of religious life, that the aggressive individualism of the recent more liberal years has infected the way religious now view this vow.

From 'I' to 'We'

The decisive shift in obedience that came with Vatican II called us to study and read the signs of the times. This moved obedience from the small world of endless permissions, which kept religious life almost at the level of infancy, to the struggle to discern God's will in the rapidly changing world in which we find ourselves. The sheer complexity of this world also undermines the simplistic claim that superiors had a kind of hot line to God. One of the consequences of this is that no one individual today can read the signs of the times alone. It helps to shift the emphasis from I to We as noted in the chapter on community.

The question as to how obedience relates to postmodern culture is an interesting one. At one level there seems to be an unbridgeable gap. After some of the horrors of the twentieth century, authority of any kind is in retreat. An essential part of the postmodern critique is to uncover and reject any dominant power or clique that excludes or marginalises any group in its interpretation of reality. At the same time there is a distinct turning towards the more subjective inner relational world. Postmodernism is trying to bring reason and feeling into a more productive relationship:

Creative postmodernity, in this way, is a new sensibility that aims at wholeness. It sees modernity as having caused an abyss between the rational and the subjective aspects of humanity, by developing both dimensions in isolation from one another.[77]

The difficulty however is that postmodernity also rejects any attempt at a *meta-story*, any attempt to provide a coherent explanation. This might seem to close the door on Christianity or any other faith that tries to provide a worldview.

---

[77] Michael P Gallagher *Clashing Symbols* p 94

A Humbler Role

While it might appear that this attitude prevents any conversation with Christianity, I think that the current numerical decline being experienced in the Church and western religious life offers the opportunity of a new, much humbler, role for religious. One of the notable shifts in ministry in recent years may offer this kind of opportunity. This shift marks a change from an older model of training. Previously formation emphasised knowledge and skills to be passed on to others through the work of ministry. Today the emphasis has changed to include, not just sharing *what one knows*, but also sharing *who one is*. That is why it is so vital for the minister to take responsibility for the inner as well as the outer journey. Not many people in our postmodern world are impressed just by ideas however well presented; they don't want *answers*. There is a deep suspicion of such answers. It is important that those involved in pastoral ministry share their struggles, weaknesses and limitations. They want to see us as wounded healers rather than superior people who know it all. If we want to *talk the talk* we have to *walk the walk*. A humbler approach will require genuine listening, and lead to a more compassionate and less judgmental ministry. Unfortunately the masculine left-brain mentality is still strong; perhaps the decline in religious vocations may work in our favour here and produce more collaborative attitudes.

Collaborative Ministry

The collaborative approach is the key to the new understanding of religious obedience. This vow needs to be rescued from the restrictive straitjacket of the past, when superiors often acted alone in interpreting God's will and *subjects* were asked to obey without question. As with all aspects of religious renewal, we have to look at the person of Jesus. We have already mentioned how the obedience to the Father, which characterised his whole mission, was demonstrated in a courageous living out of the values of the kingdom. Where the Old Testament called the people of Israel to put their lives at the service of others, Jesus takes this even further by asking his followers to be prepared to surrender their lives:

If anyone wants to be a follower of mine let him renounce himself and take up his cross every day and follow me. For

anyone who wants to save his life will lose it; but anyone who loses his life for my sake that man will save it.[78]

This issue of realigning one's will with another goes to the prophetic heart of what obedience is about. Traditional religious life placed great emphasis on the individual sacrifice; but too often it was in very small, and sometimes inhuman, ways. Think of the way religious, especially women, were denied permission to attend the funeral of a parent.

Beyond Functional Obedience

The call of Vatican II to read the signs of the times and to respect the dignity of the person has led to a more mature understanding and practice of this vow. But here also the prevailing cultural stress on masculine functional values has, if anything, restricted the prophetic nature of this vow to the area of mission alone. The job of the provincial superior is to supply personnel to get the job done; the local superior then tends to be seen in terms of a local manager. His job is seen as primarily organisational. This functional approach gravely weakens the whole purpose of obedience in the tradition of Jesus of Nazareth:

> **It is, in fact, contrary to the Christian understanding of creation that God should give us life as human persons and communities made in the image and after the likeness of God, and yet expect nothing nobler from us than the investment of our time and energy in the execution of functions. God's business as the Trinity involved actively in creation is primarily the creation and promotion of life in persons and communities.**[79]

The theology of communion, which guides the Church today, helps us to see how the whole life and growth of persons-in-community is at the centre of what God wishes to share with humanity. In the incarnation, God takes the form of human limitation and poverty. As we see in Jesus, he surrounds himself with intimate friends who share in his mission; and he invites these friends (not servants) to share this message and way of living with the whole world. Jesus commissions the group to go out and teach all nations.

A New Balance

We need a new balance in the way we live our lives. Spirituality is the way to that balance. Many commentators feel that the greatest area of neglect

---

[78] Luke 9:23-24

[79] R Kevin Seasoltz *Religious Obedience: Liberty and Law* in Philibert p 83

in our very extraverted and busy culture is the inner life. We never get the balance completely right, but it is important to see the solution here also in terms of *both/and* rather than *either/or*. There can be a real danger in seeing the inner journey as the place to rest. This is why the contemplative way is so important. The further we travel in the quest for God, the more we travel into the centre, and the more we are united with all reality. When properly balanced and lived, the two journeys become one. This is the very opposite of the fragmented nature of so much contemporary life. Our world needs heroes and heroines to find, discover and live this unity, not just for their own sakes, but for the sake of us all. This is the true purpose of religious life.

The first time Parsival enters the Grail chamber he is so distracted by the outer-surface reality of everything happening around him that he fails to ask the question; 'Whom does the Grail serve?' Later, more experienced and wiser, he gets a second chance. He has experienced failure, pain and suffering. Traditionally religion uses the word *sin*, but it can often sound rather trite and bloodless. He now knows that life doesn't *work*, it is not *fair*. People get sick, lose jobs, children get abused or exploited, marriages that began with such hopes of love and fulfilment, end in acrimony or even violence. For religious today you could point to the decline of religious life, the closing of houses, the inability to respond to the many needs, the widespread indifference to what we are about, the increasing elderly profile. Whom does the Grail serve is a question all of us need to ask from the heart.

Alignment with the Real

As Richard Rohr points out in the *Quest for the Grail* all healthy religion and spirituality eventually has to cope with blood, with pain, with suffering. When Parsival enters the Grail chamber for the second time he sees the man carrying the bleeding lance in the Grail procession. He takes the lance and gives it to the wounded fisher king who now receives the healing he needs. Parsival has now aligned himself with what is truly real:

When religion gets serious, however, it draws blood. Religion is fascinated by the sword. What was Mary told? "A sword is going to pierce your heart"(Luke 2:35). Until the sword pierces the

heart, until blood is shed, the profound thoughts are not revealed, the truth is not real. Blood in this context is the consciously allowed pain of realigning oneself with what is real.[80]

Unhealthy religion too often takes us down a variety of escape routes. We seek favours, look for miracles, religious success stories, we look for comfort in numbers of recruits and we like people telling us how good we are. We even allow religious life to play the institutional Church games of maintenance and running the system.

The Danger of the Soft Feminine

What happens then is that the heroic journey from the masculine to the feminine gets trapped in the soft feminine. I think that this is one of the most serious temptations facing religious life today. We stop asking questions. We do not rock the boat. We model the company virtues of compliance, of quiet and efficient service. We get on with our jobs because they take up enough energy anyway. In any case, it is deemed unchristian to be a source of upset and disquiet. This is the shallow obedience that all institutions tend to promote.

This is the great temptation of the soft feminine. Our mothers usually want us to be nice and to be popular. The sword which Parsival grasps is a great symbol of masculine spirituality, of the need to confront, to ask questions, to separate, to judge, to evaluate. As with all Christian spirituality, Mary is the great symbol of maturity and balance. Traditionally we have done the figure of Mary no favours by reducing her life to a story of quiet, unassuming, soft feminine virtues. We have left her with silver hands. Her very heart, the core of her being, is pierced by the sword. Mary's Magnificat is a wonderful example of a balanced spirituality: the humility and lowliness of the handmaid, combined with the vision of a new world, in which the Lord will put down the mighty and send the rich away empty. Thankfully, in religious life today, there are some very courageous and prophetic women who are prepared to ask the question, "Whom does the Grail serve?" Sadly these brave sisters are often most ridiculed by male religious and priests, as we men continue to deny our shadow.

---

[80] Richard Rohr *Quest for the Grail* (N Y Crossroad Publishing Company 1994) p 142

Nevertheless there are significant numbers of women in religious life who are prepared to be spiritual warriors, and are integrating their feminine and masculine selves. As women have engaged with the outer journey, and entered the largely patriarchal competitive world, they see the need to bring the relational side of themselves into a more integrated whole. While not neglecting their own needs as women, they can work towards a more inclusive and collaborative style:

This is the sacred marriage of the feminine and the masculine – when a woman can truly serve not only the needs of others but can value and be responsive to her own needs as well. This focus on integration and the resulting awareness of interdependence is necessary for each one of us at this time as we work together to preserve the balance of life on earth.[81]

St Paul tells us that in assuming the limitations of our humanity Christ:

was humbler yet, even to accepting death, death on a cross.[82]

Our egos inevitably struggle with the need to re-align ourselves with that kind of saviour. At root this is the sacrifice that a life of obedience calls for. We have to re-align ourselves with God's agenda for the world, rather than our own individualistic concerns. Obedience can never be reduced to a private agenda, not even to a Church agenda; it places us in line with God's will, which is God's dream for humanity. So we read history, God's story for humanity, together. We discern the action of the Spirit in the signs of the times together.

Healthy Planning

One way in which post-conciliar religious life has tried to respond to this challenge is in the whole area of planning. Such planning together helps to promote mutual shared responsibility for community and province life. It recognises the complexity of situations that face us in a rapidly changing world. It promotes a genuine sense that we are co-creators with the Holy Spirit, in the building of the Kingdom. It tries to honour everybody's gifts and insights in the discerning of God's will. It strives to translate vision into practice, and we need both. Life today is so complex and deeply connected that if we don't plan someone else will be planning for us.

---

81 Maureen Murdoch *The Heroine's Journey* (Boston Shambhala Publications 1990) p 11

82 Philippians 2:8

I have criticised old-style religious obedience for being too narrowly focussed. Planning too can also end up in this trap. We have to strive to ensure that our plans really do try to meet the real hungers of the age. It is particularly important that religious don't turn inwards in their planning. Today more than ever we must plan with the laity in a genuinely collaborative style. Sometimes religious find this difficult. In our traditional apostolates when numbers were plentiful we always had control. Now with fewer numbers this is becoming more difficult. Rather than bemoan this development we must embrace it as we plan alongside lay colleagues. True collaborative ministry really does demand the death of our egos; and we have seen how difficult that can be.

When we turn to the agenda of our 21st Century world the issues can be daunting: world poverty, pollution of the planet, the problem of refugees and asylum seekers, violence, the growth of fundamentalism, the threat of terrorism, the fear of biological, chemical or nuclear attack, the breakdown of family life, the drug culture, abortion, teenage pregnancies, the list goes on. In the face of all these problems we can easily lose hope. We cannot resolve these issues; all we can do is to be faithful wherever we find ourselves and try to identify some area that we can respond to.

From Change to Transformation

I don't think it is our task to change the world. Our task, as followers of Jesus, is to transform ourselves and hopefully in the process invite others to do the same. What matters, in the heroic journey, is not so much reaching the goal, but making the journey. Learning to integrate everything that happens to us as we encounter what is truly real. We are not Messiahs. What Jesus seems to be looking for is men and women who are willing to carry the mystery in themselves, the mystery of light and dark, of the outer and the inner, of the masculine and the feminine, of joy and pain, of tears and laughter. That is the Paschal Mystery.

Religious observers of our postmodern world have pointed to the signs of interest in what can very broadly be called the spiritual. This interest in spirituality has grown, as interest in organised religion has declined.[83] What results is a very privatised view of spirituality, one with a kind of pick-n-mix approach. Such spirituality is unlikely to engage in anything

83 Diarmuid O'Murchu *Reclaiming Spirituality* (Dublin Gill and Macmillan Ltd 1997)

prophetic or challenging. Healthy religion keeps spirituality grounded in the real, with real imperfect people in real imperfect communities, with common rituals that keep us in touch with the wider symbolic landscape.

The Bigger Picture

The problem is that with the collapse of the meta-story, the rejection of what was traditionally called the Great Chain of Being, that ancient sense that everything was integrated, we have lost the symbolic universe. There is no coherent narrative left that binds us all together, and we are wandering aimlessly in the flatlands. The individual, standing alone, is the only reference point. Consumer choice is the great entitlement. We yearn for relationships, but cannot sustain them. The consumer society tries to meet our deep emotional needs by offering us more and more things to satisfy our hunger. Because our pain and disillusionment is so deep, we project deep cynicism on to all who are involved in the political process, as we are endlessly entertained by technically sophisticated media.

Throughout its history, religious life has attempted to find ways of responding to the crisis of the age. In the third and fourth century Antony and Pachomius led Christians out into the deserts of Egypt to find God. In the middle ages Dominic and Francis led others out into the marketplaces in a changing European society. In the eighteenth and nineteenth century men and women like John Baptist de la Salle, Julie Billiart, John Bosco, and many others responded to the need to provide education as industrialisation created new urban poor. This work tended to stay within the Catholic community. I am not suggesting that we neglect this work, its need is as real as ever, but I do think we can widen our vision. What are the new hungers of the twenty first century?

If postmodernism tells us anything it seems to demand that we do not allow any one group to hijack the common debate. Perhaps the one group that we fear most at this time is the stranger, those of other faiths and other cultures. The word religion is from the Latin re–ligio, to bind together. This is the contribution of healthy religion in any age. The world has probably stopped listening to us because so much of what we have been saying has been coming out of the left-brain heavily masculine framework of winners and losers, who is right and who is wrong. It is all about control.

The stranger is always the one who threatens my worldview and the needs of my ego control. I began this book by reflecting on a recent visit to Ground Zero in New York City, a harrowing symbol of what happens when fanaticism and fundamentalism lashes out in anger. In the area of North West England, where I have lived in recent years, we have had street riots between racial groups. Government reports into these disorders commented that in our different communities, religious or otherwise, we lead parallel lives. If spirituality is about seeing, and the need to keep cleansing the lens with prayer and humble service, then maybe we religious can open our minds and our hearts, and even our communities, to the stranger, to those of other faiths and traditions so that we can begin a dialogue and a narrative that includes rather than excludes. In this way we can respond to the challenge of Jesus:

I was a stranger and you made me welcome.[84]

If we are to do this we must, of course, begin by welcoming the stranger within. The journey without, which takes us into the heart of our contemporary world, always takes us back within, into our hearts. Apostolic religious life has always promoted the primacy of action, of moving into the world with a sense of daring and risk, and of encounter with the disadvantaged. This *obedience* to the dream of God for mankind moves us into a depth experience of our poverty of spirit. There, in contemplation like Mary, we ponder these things in our hearts, which are then transformed by a compassionate love and mercy.

[84] Matthew 25:35

Two Become One

Our whole Christian life must be a back and forth between the radical way inward and the radical way outward.[85]

The city of San Francisco has two beautiful cathedrals. While visiting the modern Roman Catholic Cathedral of St Mary's I was struck by the two large clear glass windows behind the main altar, one of which looks out onto the skyline of downtown San Francisco, while the other is angled towards the hills that encircle the beautiful City by the Bay. For me this sacred space strongly underlines the fact that prayer and worship are not meant to take us out of the world. It situates us more firmly in what is real, in this case the beauty and bustle of a great city.

The Labyrinth

From there I crossed to the more traditional Grace Episcopal Cathedral. As I entered the building the first thing that caught my eye was a group of people walking silently and thoughtfully in a circular motion at the foot of the great gothic nave. They were walking the labyrinth which has been set up there by Lauren Artress, Canon Pastor of the Cathedral.[86] The labyrinth is an ancient mystical tool that has long been used across the centuries as a metaphor for the spiritual journey. The canvas labyrinth at Grace Cathedral is modelled exactly on what was laid down in Chartres Cathedral in the twelve century. A labyrinth is not a maze. A maze engages the thinking mind, the labyrinth engages the intuitive side of the mind. The movement is into the centre and back out again. It offers the opportunity to walk both the inner and outer journey.

Much of our western civilisation has been shaped by the classical myths of Greece and Rome. Achilles conquers Troy wearing a labyrinth on his breastplate. Perseus attacks Medusa with a labyrinth on his shield. The labyrinth points to the complexity of life and the fact that progress is rarely linear as the great myth of modernity tried to suggest. When Theseus kills the Minotaur he exits the labyrinth using a piece of string, a symbol of soul wisdom given to him by a woman.

---

85 Richard Rohr *Simplicity* (N Y Crossroad Publishing Company 1997) p 100

86 For a fuller explanation of the labyrinth as a spiritual path see Dr Lauren *Artress Walking a Sacred Path* (N Y Riverhead Books 1995). See also Richard Rohr *Quest for the Grail* (N Y Crossroad Publishing Company 1997) pp 34-36

The labyrinth is part of the great Christian tradition of pilgrimage. Our postmodern world has made tourism one of its growth industries and it is interesting to see how international terrorism is now focussing on this soft target. While holidays are important times for rest and relaxation they rarely touch us at a deep level. In contrast the great Christian tradition has promoted the idea of pilgrimage as a metaphor for life's journeys and transformations. A tourist tends to take a detached interest, while the pilgrim is engaged at a deeper level in the whole experience. The labyrinth is part of that wisdom tradition, and it is a perfect symbol of the two journeys, the inner and the outer which are in fact one journey.

To walk the labyrinth it is necessary to close down the superficial concerns that often tire our minds and spirits, to create a calm and reflective mood, to quiet what the Buddhists call the *monkey mind*, swinging restlessly from branch to branch. We have to let go of our restless thoughts as in centring or contemplative prayer. The journey into the centre of the labyrinth is walked slowly and meditatively. It contains twists and turns as in life but all of them lead eventually to the centre. It can take as long as you wish.

The centre of the labyrinth takes us to the core of the within, the sacred space of the heart, where our true self is hidden in God. It is a time to simply be aware of the goodness of all reality. It is a place where the intuitive, the right brain, takes over from the analytical left brain. At the centre the pilgrim simply waits for the message to emerge from within.

Just as it is impossible to stay forever in a Grail experience, so too the pilgrim must now begin the outer journey, the journey without. This too has its twists and turns but the whole walk reminds us of the importance of the path. Our capitalist, competitive minds are so hung up on achievement, on getting somewhere, on success. This even infects our prayer life as we struggle to measure our progress. The labyrinth connects us with a deeper soul-wisdom that reminds us that it is the travelling that matters not the arriving.

The Contemplative Vision

As we move into the twenty first century the future of religious life is far from clear. In a time of transition and change, the temptation is to find answers quickly and get on with the action agenda. But if we are being invited to move into the sacred feminine, the place of soul wisdom, we need to move from the calculating mind to the contemplative one.

The contemplative mind invites us to rejoice in the unconditional love of God. Eternal life is now, Jesus tells us. Whatever is happening to us is all part of the good news: God is present to us in a completely non-blaming way. While we worry about trying to change people, God seems to have the most amazing patience and respect for the complexity of every individual, and invites us to walk the path in the enchanted labyrinth of life.

Its twists and turns will take us into many challenges and setbacks revealing a God, who as Father, demands our growth into commitment, and a God who, as Mother, offers us radical acceptance and forgiving love experienced in the core of our being. We cannot fix the problems we see all around us; that is the action of the calculating mind. The contemplative mind embraces life in all its aspects, the good, the bad and the ugly. Instead of trying to fix others all we are asked to do is to enter into the joys and sorrows of life and allow them to transform us.

We do not yet know the contours of this exciting and challenging postmodern age. It is up to our generation, and others maybe, to shape it and give it a human face, to discover meaning in the struggle for human values. This is a spiritual task. It demands spiritual men and women who are alive to the deepest purpose of human life: to discover and witness to the great love story between God and humanity. The practices and structures of spiritual and religious life exist only to prepare us for moments of profound awareness of this mystery, which can happen in a burning bush, on Mount Tabor, or even, most mysteriously of all, in places of human suffering, in the Calvarys of this world:

> **I imagine that I walk into a desert place.**
> **I spend some time exploring the surroundings,**
> **then settle down to contemplate my life.**
> **I see how frequently I rush outside myself**
> **- to people, occupations, places, things -**
> **in search of strength and peace and meaning,**
> **forgetting that the source of all**
> **is here within my heart.**
> **It is here that I must search.**[87]

[87] Anthony de Mello *Wellsprings* (N Y Image Books 1986) p 31